Mount Zion Field

Scripta Humanistica

Directed by
BRUNO M. DAMIANI
The Catholic University of America

ADVISORY BOARD

Mount Zion Field

J. Thomas O'Connell

$\mathfrak{Scripta\ humanistica}$

33

O'Connell, J. Thomas,
    Mount Zion Field

    (Scripta humanistica; 33)
    I. Title.   II. Series.
PS3565.C525M6   1987   813'.54   87-9543
ISBN 0-916379-39-6

                    Publisher and Distributor:
                    SCRIPTA HUMANISTICA
                    1383 Kersey Lane
                    Potomac, Maryland 20854 U.S.A.

Acknowledgements

There are many persons and organizations I would like to acknowledge that contributed to the preparation of this manuscript. The American Guide Series Writer's Program volume on Alabama is not only interesting but was invaluable and Neil Pierce told me much about Alabama as well as about himself. The Alabama Archives, the Alabama Historical Society, and the United Daughters of the Confederacy are repositories rich in knowledge that made themselves readily available to any and all questions. The librarians and staff of the Davis Library in Montgomery County, Maryland produced volumes and scraps of paper I never imagined existed. The Justice Department, the Attorney General offices of numerous states and the Historical Division of the NAACP also responded as requested as did the Historical Division of the U.S. Department of the Army.

Then there were others, Judge Perry Bowen, and Tom Henry of the Washington Star; friends Peter Schissler, Gene Watson, Bill O'Connell and Charles Geschickter, who told me about doctors and lawyers and what they do; these, as well as Bernie Dooley, read and made many valuable suggestions to this work.

To all of them, my gratitude and best wishes.

J. Thomas O'Connell

CHARACTERS

John Prichard	— the prosecutor
Jenny Holcombe Prichard	— John's wife
Thomas Newbold	— the judge
Comfort Newbold	— the judge's wife
Jack Farakshnt	— a journalist
William Marmande	— defense counsel
Newton Christy	— the doctor
Wardel Mackel	— the victim
Ross Brooks	— the defendant
Jeremiah Crowley	— a F.B.I. agent
Redtop	— the sheriff
Jack Hawes	— a deputy
Franklin Day	— an employee of John Prichard's father
Cora	— Franklin's daughter
Warren Lankford	— the coroner
Charles Pith	— a witness
Dewey Bishop	— a friend
Justice of the Peace Charles	— a lower magistrate
Turpin Ellis	— a juror

Chapter One

Tallawampa is laid out in squares or grids. There are 20 of these squares or grids, the centrally placed squares being symmetrical and the peripherally located ones, those that spill over into the proximate countryside, being asymmetrical. The population of Tallawampa is 1,015. The town slopes very gradually towards the southwest; so gradual, in fact, that you notice it only when you walk eastward and then there is a barely perceptible rise. The curbs on the north side of the streets are also slightly higher than those on the southern side of the streets. Eccentric to the center of town, that is slightly to the east, is the courthouse. It is here that the judicial disputes of Tallawampa are resolved; most of these are of a minor nature. It has been over two years since there has been a murder trial here. From the courthouse's second and top floor you can see over most of the city. This building was built of red brick and is recessed from the street it faces by a lawn of blue grass that is protected by an incomplete awning of trees. A bi-concave walkway made of similar bricks as the courthouse extends from the sidewalk of the street across the lawn to the portico of this building. Near the point of greatest concavity in the walkway is a statue commemorating Alabama's 23rd Infantry Regiment from the Civil War, as well as two plaques, one commemorating the 167th Regiment of the Rainbow Division in World War I and the other plaque commemorates the same Alabama regiment that participated in the Dixie Division in World War II. These three Bronzes are fixed in marble and granite.

Three broad stone steps rise from the brick walkway to the por-

1

tico of the building which is covered by an extension of the courthouse roof. The roof of the portico is supported by four unfluted oval columns each with three-tiered concentric moldings at their capitals and bases. The portico or gallery extends the full length of the building and is 20 feet in depth. From its floor a single step rises to the door of the building. This door is made of thick hard wood and is painted a gloss white; it has two parallel halves but only the right side opens. The sheer size of this movable portion of the door causes difficulty in pushing it open. To this difficulty is added the knob of the door's simple ward lock that so imprecisely moves its bolt that there is always an additional delay in opening. The door closes quickly by its own weight.

Inside the building there is a central foyer and from this extend three corridors at right angles to each other. If you take the corridor to the left, that is, the one that goes north, you pass the office of the probate judge with its wills and licenses, the tax assessor's office, the county engineer and the board of commissioners. The opposite corridor leading southward takes you past the offices of the superintendent of education, the selective service office, the tax collector's office, and the offices for the clerk of the circuit court. The third corridor, that is, the extension of the foyer to the back of the building, leads you past walls decorated with murals depicting the harvest and history of the county. These include scenes of cotton choppers and a cotton gin, a prehistoric Indian mound, the anti-bellum home Melwood, a beef farm, and forestry. At the end of this corridor you ascend a centrally placed stairway that rises to a landing between the two floors of the building. From this landing you may walk down a bare masonry corridor that continues to the rear of the building. This corridor is guarded by a secured, lockable door. The opposite end of this masonry corridor has a similar door and here Sheriff Redtop has his office. With Sheriff Redtop's office is a communications room as well as a room for a deputy, a clerk, a ward room for whatever intent is needed, and a jailer, if occasion demands. Beyond these rooms are three cells, each separate but leading into a common barren enclosure measuring 20 by 20 feet. Sheriff Redtop was elected to keep his jail empty.

At the landing between the two floors of the courthouse you can continue up either of two laterally placed stairs that return you toward the front of the building. These stairs enter into an expanded

2

portion of the second floor corridor. This corridor runs the length of the building north and south dividing the building into front and back portions. Across from the stairs at the expanded portion of the corridor is the entrance to Alabama's first circuit court. Visitors entering the courtroom are in the spectators' gallery facing the judge's bench. Stained wood railings, tables, chairs and benches give the room a rough handsomeness. The walls are painted antique white and the vaulted ceiling has a centrally placed hexagonal glass cupola that allows in light. The thick lead glass panes of the cupola faintly and irregularly disperse the light into its spectrum.

To the right of the judge's bench is a desk for a court reporter as well as a bench, table, and chairs for the prosecution. Also to the right is a door leading to the judge's chambers. These chambers are in the southwest corner of the building. To the left of the judge's bench is the witness stand, the jury box and table with chairs for the defense. Beyond the jury box is a door leading into the room where the jurors deliberate. This room is in the northwest corner of the building. The courtroom, with a capacity for slightly over 200 people, was the largest room in the county until the new auditorium of the school was built; it would take a spectacular trial to fill it with so many.

The back portion of the second floor of the courthouse is divided by the central stairway. The left side as you ascend the stairwell has rooms for the bailiff, a small room to secure evidence, and a conference room for lawyers and their clients. The space on the opposite side of the stairwell contains the office of the prosecuting attorney and a small library. The office is John Prichard's. John has been the County's prosecuting attorney for slightly over 8 years. The courthouse is Tallawampa's architectural grandness and could be vaunted by other similar communities.

Returning to the portico of the courthouse you can look down First Street. On the northwest corner of First Street and Courthouse Square is Prichard's Store, or what was Prichard's Store. The faded painted sign on the second floor of the brick wall is still visible but the store was sold nearly 15 years ago to Delta Pride. That franchised retailer has perpetuated the store with its products for the people of Tallawampa. There is an entrance into Prichard's from both Courthouse Square and First Street, these two being separated by a common buttress at the corner of the building. Either entrance leads into

3

a large room that contains most of the needs for a rural agricultural community. Here you may buy feeds, fertilizers, grains, seeds, hoses, lanterns, rakes, hammers, ladders, paints, plumbing fixtures, cloths, dresses, hats, shirts, shoes, and other things necessary for field, barnyard, home and person. John Prichard's father and his hired helper, Franklin Day, spent hours and years in this store waiting on all of Tallawampa as they passed through this place on multiple buying days or weekly Saturday shopping trips. John had worked in the store on afternoons and Saturdays, as well as parts of summers, waiting first on his father and Franklin and later directly on customers. There was no place in Tallawampa more visible than Prichard's. You could watch the whole community from that store.

Across the street on the southwest corner of First and Courthouse Square are the law offices of Noone, Creek and Pardoe. Moore, Wilson and Moore have their offices next to the other three. These six gentlemen serve the legal needs of the tri-county area, and one of them is frequently in town. They probate the wills, record the deeds, and attend to the other legal needs in the area, as well as handling any criminal cases that may occur. Next to Prichard's on the same side of First Street is Mellon's Restaurant. Mellon's is actually only half restaurant, the other half being a cafeteria with a food and soda counter. Mellon's is almost as old as Prichard's. It is the only real public eating place in Tallawampa. It has six tables in the dining room that looks out a large window allowing customers to view the activities of First Street. The Mellons serve the kitchen and counter while a single waitress serves the dining room. Continuing down First Street there are other essential small businesses that support the community. An insurance office, the bank, the drugstore, the grammar and high schools, the library, a beauty shop, the farm bureau, the garage with a gas station, a funeral parlor, and other establishments that make up the commercial portion of town. Only Mellons and the gas station welcome occasional out-of-towners.

At the end of First Street on the western boundary of town is Semmes Street. If you turn left here and go down two blocks, you come to John Prichard's house. It is a white multi-gabled Victorian house surrounded by a generous lawn. There is a half porch on the front of the house and this enters into a small foyer off of which is a dining room and kitchen on the one side, and a parlor and living room on the other side. It's the kitchen and living room that John

4

and Jenny use most. Upstairs there are four bedrooms—one shared by John and Jenny, one used for storage, and one for a study, and one unused. The house, John and Jenny, wait for the use of that extra room. Still further down Semmes Street the road continues into the country and passes the Methodist cemetery. John's parents and grandparents are buried there. Jenny's family is from Grove Hill.

At the other end of Semmes Street, that is, the northern end, there is the river. By the time the river has reached Tallawampa it has picked up a sufficient number of streams and creeks to have formed one of the large dendrites of the Tombigbee. As the river passes Tallawampa it forms a crest that bends toward town so that the deeper and faster portion of the river is adjacent to the city. This depth of the river allows Tallawampa to have a wharf and dock. In days past freight was frequent on the river and times before that passenger traffic was not uncommon. The piers and their warehouse (a liberal designation) have fallen into decay as a consequence of disuse ever since the county's cotton harvest has been transported to market by other means.

When you return to First and Semmes Street you can look back at the courthouse or to the continuation of First Street into the country where it is now called Bashan Road. This road winds and extends past farms and country communities ultimately dissipating itself in impinging foliage and by the river that has already turned and headed south. The farms here vary; most are orderly and of moderate size. A few are small and fewer are large. Cotton, soybean and cattle are the principal crops. The colored communities along Bashan Road are made up of small unpainted wooden houses with tin roofs. These houses are grouped irregularly about small bleached white frame churches. It is these churches that are the principal support for these communities. Other houses extend down secondary and tertiary roads.

One of these collections of people is supported by Mount Zion Church, a rectangular wooden structure with an oval stained glass window over its door. The panes of glass are red and green with a light perpetually shining from behind them. Next to Mt. Zion's church is Tangent Road which rambles off to the southwest to a lightly timbered area that contains a ball field and a picnic area for the church. As you approach this field by the dirt road you enter just behind home plate, which is protected by a backstop made of chicken wire

5

supported by wooden poles. The infield is a fine powdered dust or mud depending upon the most recent rain. The foul lines are obliterated by the dust or mud. The outfields are covered by tall sunburnt grasses. Along the first and third base lines there are two weathered splintered benches for players; behind the third base line bench are four rows of stands of similar construction and condition for perhaps 25 spectators. Not far from the stands is a stone barbecue grill. The playing field is unlevel, right field slanting uphill. Trees impinge on left field sooner than right and a shot into left field reaches the woods more quickly and is an easier home run. The incline and distance to right field make it more difficult to hit well too. The deepest portion of right field continues as an abandoned logger's road into the forest. No one wanders onto that road.

On inspection there is abundant drabness at Mount Zion field. It is without color, taste or flavor. It is bland and burnt; but this physical blandness should not be interpreted that it is a place without mirth. Thousands of softballs have careened off the powdered infield and cut through the withered grasses of the outfields amid the whoops and hollers of youths draped with the plummage of bats and gloves, before the flutters of hearts and under the surveillance of elders. Season after season children have grown to adulthood and maturity at Mount Zion's field.

When you return to Bashan Road from Mount Zion field you can continue on away from town to other communities and farms. One of these farms is "Somerset" where Judge Thomas Newbold lives.

Back in town behind the courthouse to the east is Tallawampa's industrial district. The railroad formed the heart of this portion of town when long ago it replaced the river as the principal means of transportation. The tracks run north and south and form the eastern boundary of town. They connect Tallawampa to Montgomery, Birmingham, and ultimately Memphis to the north; they continue south to Mobile. Once there was sufficient passenger and freight to warrant a stationmaster for the occasional selling of tickets and for the recording of shipments and other documents necessary for commerce. However, travel on the railroad has declined just as on the river before it; now no passengers are seen and the passenger cars have long since disappeared from the trains. The marked decrease in the utilization of the train even for freight has required any paper work needed for commerce to be performed by the attendants of the train and the recipients of the services themselves. But the freight that is still shipped (cotton, cattle and lumber) necessitate the small buildings, yards, and pens needed to protect these goods from the weather and other elements. With the continued decline in railroad use the local railroad position has been demoted from stationmaster to clerk, and finally to yard attendant. Ross Brooks is the current yard attendant. It is Ross with his friends who make up Tallawampa's small industrial tenant population. Most members of this group commute during the week to Montgomery to lesser jobs or occasionally remain in Tallawampa to work at odd tasks. The few remaining members of the group are young vagrants from the adjoining countryside. This coterie of friends is of unpredictable transiency but while in residence they support the local arcade and eatery that provides relief for occasional truckers and buses. Ross and his friends struggle with life, a struggle most of them will lose.

Parallel to the train tracks is alternate state Route 24. This highway also comes down from the north and brings nearly all of the commerce, traffic, trade and people to Tallawampa. The road used to run along the northern edge of town, turn south and go through the heart of town past the courthouse, and then exit into the country. But with the addition of larger trucks and greater use of the road an alternate route was built to bypass the center of town. This new road continues along with the railroad tracks skirting Tallawampa to the east to join the old road south of town. There the two continue as one before dividing, one branch going to Mobile and the other to Mississippi.

If you were to identify a single cause for change in Tallawampa, it would be Route 24. It has been down this worn and frayed state road that nearly everything new has come to the area; changes never imagined. It easily has had the greatest impact. In fact, without Route 24 there would be no changes at all. Tallawampa would be as it always was, isolated, nearly landlocked deep in the recesses of the continent, enveloped by moats of agricultural earth that produced the necessities of life but little more. These moats were crossed by few going out and even fewer coming in. It was over this tertiary road that the changes came, slowly at first but with ever increasing variety, volume and rapidity.

There were all sorts of new things brought; new pieces of equip-

7

ment, new colors, shapes, clothes, music, new signs, new fabrics, appliances, cars, utensils, everything new; and each new product brought a greater demand for other new products and more new services. It was over Route 24 that the first television set came to town. It sat in Prichard's Store and for special events the men congregated at the store while others watched from outside. It was John's job to put the set on the table and to remove it to its place of safekeeping when the viewing was over. But this monopoly on the new wonder didn't last long. There was an exponential increase in the number of sets. First two, then four, then eight, then sixteen sets appeared until ultimately every battered frame hovel had a television with an antenna so that the humblest abode had a metallic eye and ear reaching for the signals of life.

Over this same road came the first flood of weekly magazines. Not magazines devoted to pictures but real magazines with articles; real articles with news events, national and international affairs, education, religion, drama, theatre, books, covering every topic you could imagine. It was these two, the magazines and the television; they didn't open windows and doors, they blew open the whole town. There was a gush of freshness that blew through town that could change all and any direction of person and things. They brought a new richness and character; they transformed Tallawampa, with new freedoms, interests, activities and horizons. They changed conversations, orientations, and awareness. They brought new dialogues; there was a new literary guild and trips for the ladies; sports and international politics (as never before) for the men. This plethora of communication brought new discussions never known before and everyone talked and participated.

"Thank God, no more, no more weather. I'm so sick and tired of talking about the weather, wondering whether those clouds will have some rain or not, whether the day is going to be warmer than yesterday, whether it is going to be cool this evening; thank God, we're finished with that! No more talking about the weather. We have so many things, so many things to see and do. Why last month we went to the Rose Bowl. Can you imagine being right there in California, and we saw all these parades and bands."

"Parades and bands, did you see that boy run, did you see that boy throw that ball, did you see that tackle?" It was incredible! Brilliant dashes to goal lines and aerial bombs that caused endless defeat without destruction.

"The Rose Bowl? California? Why, who cares about California—I saw them advertising trips to Paris! That's right, Paris, France—they call it the 'Parisian Special'—$525.00 round trip!"

"The Parisian Special?"

"That's right, the 'Parisian Special' and luxury food on the aircraft roundtrip. We're gonna go, too."

That night in numerous homes in Tallawampa could be heard the whispers of man and wife, "Why we could probably do that, we could probably do something like that. Of course, we'd have to plan; we'd have to save."

"Do you really think we could!" It seemed there was no end to the wonderment.

All sorts of marvelous things. "I saw them rounding up steers out west in a helicopter!"

"In a helicopter, what for?"

"Why they use it instead of a truck or a jeep."

"Well, if that isn't something!"

Documentaries, senators, discussions, educators, ambassadors, analysts, "Why, I didn't know it was like that." Editorials, in fact, it was like a novel and each week you waited for the news that was going on in your world and each night you could watch on T.V. the vivid pictures by scintillations of telemetry that allowed you to look into the whole world.

That year everyone in the state, including everyone in Tallawampa, went to the Orange Bowl.

"Sixty-one to six! Whoee! Did we give them a lickin'."

"Well, those fellows won't be back again, that's for sure."

"I don't think we should play them again," another one whispered.

Everyone watched the game, everyone could see it. Everyone seemed to take the changes in stride. There was no awkwardness or stumbling with the new changes; it was almost like a process of evolution—so natural and with a continuing update on activities nicely indexed and broken down into categories, readily available, easy to follow.

"We don't know the county, we know all of Alabama."

"Honey, we don't know Alabama, we know the whole world and we've never left home!"

Spectaculars, entertainment, pantomine, magic, culture, art, prize fights, you met people you had never known, people in Washington, people from all parts of the country, and from difference parts of the world. There were so many analyses of all the events and changes, everything so nicely explained.

"Did you see that prize fight?"

"You know I never saw a prize fight in my life until they started those on T.V., and boy, do those fellows pack a whallop! I mean a real prize fight. I've seen grudge fights before but I've never seen a real prize fight."

But there were occasional stories of things that had happened before that hadn't been widely publicized. Now when similar incidents occurred they were quickly focused on and extensively reported. One of those was the abduction of Moses Jones. That misfortune and calamity caused embarrassment and wasn't too far from home. "Well, it's regrettable, but what's done is done."

And then one day it was reported the Supreme Court ruled you couldn't have segregated schools. "Why, that's the silliest thing I've ever heard of!"

"Integrated schools, they say."

"Well, how are they going to integrate schools in Alabama, Texas, Tennessee, Florida, Mississippi and everywhere else? That's the dumbest thing I ever heard of."

"You mean to tell me all this time it's been right and now it's wrong?"

"That doesn't make it the law of the land, it makes it the law in those four cases, and just 'cuz some Supreme Court Justice says you have to take somebody into your school is nonsense."

"I'm tired of listening to those yappin' idiots anyway—who cares. Did you know that they have central air conditioning now. Can you imagine air conditioning the whole house with just one machine and it keeps it real nice and cool in every room."

"We don't even have a window unit yet!" whispered another.

"Electric typewriters!"

"I don't know how they know what to type; I've never seen one before but we're going to get one."

"Did you see what that lady in Mississippi called them, 'nine nincompoops!' Hee hee."

"The state legislature resolved that the Supreme Court ruling was null and void so it doesn't apply to us anyways. We're going to have a placement board where students are going to be placed where they're needed. Enough of these distractions and interruptions. There are other things to do and this year we're going to the Sugar Bowl—Navy's playing Mississippi."

"For Navy to beat Ole Miss they'll have to have more than desire." The game was played under established rules and before traditional sitting arrangements.

"Now the Supreme Court says the parks and recreational areas can't be segregated!"

"Well, we'll just close down the parks and recreation facilities and nobody will go to them and that will be the end of that. The old governor will show them."

But enough of these unpleasantries, there were nicer things to do, new people to meet, new things and new events to see. There were more books and more shows, and this fall they all decided to go to the World Series. "That's right, we're going to the World Series. No, not in New York, right here in Tallawampa, Luraline. Now I know how you feel about Yankees but they say he's from Oklahoma anyway. And we're going to have a celebration right here and watch the whole thing and we'll have a marvelous time."

Then one day in Montgomery, of all silly things, some woman wouldn't move further back in the bus and they started a boycott. "A boycott! So let them walk, they'll soon enough get sick and tired of that. And all these meetings and all those carryings on."

"Well, they say it's only the uppity ones that are involved in it anyway, that the nice ones aren't."

"I think it is disgraceful some people helping them, driving them around to work and everything."

"Well, how's someone supposed to get their house clean if they can't ride the buses and it's too far to walk to their house."

"I don't care where they're sitting on the bus, who rides the buses anyway."

"My sister Sybil needs her Lucy four days a week, and if she wants to help her and drive her, that's nobody's business but her own."

This bitterness dragged on and unpleasantries persisted. Then one day a boy was killed in Mississippi. "Well, he must have done something terribly wrong for them to have done that."

11

"He was only 14," one of them murmured as silence prevailed.

Each hot summer faded into an autumn of contention, that renewed the uneasiness of all citizens as every student marched off to their designated place of assignment.

"Enough of this, I'm tired of it all. This year we're going to have a New Year's Eve party, and Helen says we're going to dance to Guy Lombardo! That's right, right here at home! And we're going to have champagne, and we're going to party all night. They say he plays at the fanciest parties up North."

"Did you see Liz Taylor the other night? She is so lovely, I just think she's the prettiest thing, and what she sees in that puny little fella I'll never know."

"Well, they say he promised her everything."

"Lord, what could he promise her?" The weeks passed with multiple activities that consumed time and thought.

"Do you know that one of those girls wants to go to the university!"

"Well, if there ever was a chocolate chip in with sugar cookies, she'd be it! Lord, can you imagine!"

"Why do they want to go where they're not wanted? That's what I can't understand."

"Well, they're not coming in here!"

"A spade? Why Luraline, where's your southern blood? I bid two hearts! I'll take mine straight on the rocks—Pepsi with no water! Hee hee."

And every day and every week they watched and read and read and watched. The optical flashes brought home vividly the daily and weekly events and changes, the newities now so numerous that they produced a fatigue even in the stronger ones. There seemed to be no end to the rapidity with which they came, but elements of defensiveness and rigidity were being established. There was also a determination to win and in some to destroy.

But most were still buoyed up by the new wonders that brought delights. "Did you see that boy hit that ball last night. He hardly swung the bat. I never saw a boy hit a ball like that, and the other fellow—he ran clear into the wall. I told my son Phillip you put one of those boys in front of a bunch of screaming and hollerin people and they're liable to do anything, but, Phillip, that doesn't mean he's better. You know I never saw a major league baseball game until I was

35. I've seen Class AA ball games before, down in Mobile, but never a big league game."

But the unrest that persisted was not only here, there was unrest elsewhere; there were confrontations of antagonistic groups in Europe, turning over established orders, tanks in the streets. "You can see them firing into the crowds. And all those people involved, they're not going to stand for it any longer over there."

"You can't blame them, these are exciting times."

"Well, what I don't understand is, why do they advertise all those fighter bombers and missiles in the magazines. Who buys fighter bombers or missiles? David doesn't and nobody in our family does and why do they advertise those warships—who buys a battleship?"

"Lucille, the President reads that magazine," one of the more knowing responded.

"The President reads it! Well, why don't they just call on him and sell those things to him? Why do they bother the rest of us with all that— guns, airplanes and bombers. We don't need a bomber; we need a new refrigerator."

"Lucille, that's how business is done."

"Really, seems strange to me."

"Advertising bombers in magazines is one thing but paratroopers in schools is another—that's right, paratroopers in Arkansas in the schools with rifles and bayonets. The governor sent them out to protect the city. Why it's incredible what they're doing to the schools. I never heard of such a thing as paratroopers in the schools."

"Somebody is way out of line." And there was violence, rocks, bottles, hits on the head, bombs and obscenities, the President issuing orders and a diminutive judge saying, "Integrate now."

"Now they're having a voter registration."

"Voter registration! My God—well, ask them the Tenth Amendment, that will slow them down."

"Spitting on somebody, I don't care what they're doing, you just can't justify spitting on anybody."

"I don't care what anybody says, there's no justification to mutilate somebody and then pour turpentine on them! That's barbarism."

"They're boycotting the schools in Tuskegee. These schools are going to be the death of us yet."

"The world is falling apart and there are revolutions everywhere; in Cuba, the taking over of governments and all these new countries and all of them coming into the United Nations." Every week there seemed to be a new country, "and all these black people strutting around the U.N.; all those flowing robes. You could see them on T.V., there they were, right in the White House. Can you imagine that, those fellas in the White House!"

"They're going to have a boycott in Birmingham."

"Well, that will be the end of them if they do that, God help them."

"Enough of that, we will just turn the T.V. off and we'll stop reading the magazines and we'll have our meetings and discussions and we'll discuss things intelligently and politely." At the ladies cultural society's fall meeting they discussed the emerging arts and dances.

"I thought it was lovely, fine and rather delicate," began one of the matrons.

"Fine and delicate!" fired back her daughter. "Why, Mother, her tits were hanging out!" Hot flashes quivered and vibrated off the walls as matrons perspired between flushes and blanches. One of the younger ones whispered to Jenny through immovable lips, "Gloria always had a way with words."

"Doesn't she though," responded Jenny in a barely audible voice.

In the fall unpleasant crowds filled the streets of the Crescent City spitting venomous and contemptuous remarks on small children with the worst of obscenities.

"Now look what they're putting on us, the harvest of shame."

"What am I supposed to do; I can't change my life." The uneasiness and fatigue pressed into depression with a loss in interest. "I don't like it and it's uncomfortable and it's no fun." And the following spring they had a sit-down.

"Yes, a sit-down or a sit-in or something like that. They just sit in a store at a counter and they won't move and they won't leave; they're just causing trouble and they won't let anybody else come in and sit down and buy anything. They just sit there all day and leave that night, come back the next day, just sitting at the counters causing trouble, making a nuisance of themselves. What's a man supposed to do, he just can't let them drive away his business, he has to do something."

"All those college students. Almost like a swarm of locusts, and white ones too. Now they're having prayer-ins, preach-ins, lay-ins, bury-ins, sleep-ins, golf-ins, swim-ins."

"Well, they can swim in mud, for all I care, I'm not swimming with them." There were more confrontations, more stores boycotted, more schools picketed and greater ugliness prevailed. Baseness and coarseness became commonplace while the legislatures convened to disenfranchise, held special sessions, legal maneuvers to withhold budgets, and draw new school districts. In spite of all this there was a constant banging at the door.

"I'm getting sick and tired. Now they're having a freedom ride."

"A freedom ride!" one looked in disbelief. "What's a freedom ride?"

"Well, they just sit on the bus and they go riding from town to town and they stop at all the bus stations, go in all the restaurants and in the waiting rooms and they wait until something happens trying to make a rumpus and if nothing happens they move on to someplace else."

"You mean sort of like roven flatus, it just moves around everywhere smelling up everything, is that what you mean?"

"Now you have it, Dickey boy. Hee hee."

The bus ride passed unmolested until it reached Anniston where it was overturned and set alight; there were clubbings and beatings, but the riders continued on to Birmingham and further.

"Who wants to think of this, let's watch the beautiful people. I'm telling you there's a new crowd and they're smart and they're elegant too. They're into symphonies, ballet, the theatre. They water ski, play tennis, jog, they're real athletes; and the women are beautiful, gracious; they'll set the pace—we'll have our freedom yet."

"Good God, they're bombing churches!"

"Bombing churches? Are we really that bad?" someone said with despair.

"I can't stand it, I'd rather watch the beautiful people."

"The University of Mississippi integrated!"

"I don't believe it!"

"I'm telling you the truth. Some black guy wants to go to the University of Mississippi."

"Man, I have to see this, the University of Mississippi integrated! Daddy...they're integrating Ole Miss!" And for days there were police, federal marshals, the campus strewn with bottles, debris, gas cannisters, cans, missiles, bats, clubs, confrontations, murder, F.B.I. agents, watching and checking on everyone; police dogs, dynamite! "Good God, seems like bombs are scattering everywhere!"

Tallawampa sat, and like the rest, watched the evolution taking place. They weren't sure what it meant to Tallawampa or how it would affect them. If Alabama was the heart of Dixie, Tallawampa had to be someplace in the heart's left ventricle. But there was nothing to integrate in Tallawampa and who could find it anyway and who would want to come here; in fact, Tallawampa wasn't really segregated, at least not in the sense most people mean it. The schools were segregated but most of the people in the county were colored, and if you integrated schools, you wouldn't have blacks going to white schools, you'd have whites going to black schools. Besides, that's how the schools had always been, at least since there had been public schools, and nobody seemed to care, or if they did, they didn't say anything.

John's father's store wasn't segregated; why there wasn't even a place to sit down. The colored people never tried on any of the clothes they bought, they just bought them and took the clothes with them.

John's father waited on all the whites, Franklin waited on all the colored; that's the way it was. Everyone seemed to prefer it that way; at least no one said any differently. In fact, the colored looked up to Franklin, they even called him Mister. He was certainly a leader in their community.

Mellon's Restaurant wasn't integrated, or segregated. The colored never went in there. It wasn't expensive but they couldn't afford it anyway; and God knows even they wouldn't go to that eatery near the railroad tracks. There were no hotels in Tallawampa. If you wanted to stay overnight, you had to stay in someone's home. There weren't any clubs in town either; the social activities centered about the family and the churches. The colored participated in the Fourth of July celebration and also in the county fair. The churches weren't segregated; they were just different congregations, separated as they had always been. And why would they want to pray with us? There were segregated bathrooms and drinking fountains in the courthouse

16

but as little as the colored used them theirs were probably cleaner than those used by the whites. John Prichard was a segregationist, at least he lived as a segregationist; everybody was, at least everyone in Alabama, and you couldn't have changed it if you wanted to. All this would pass and blow away it was agreed. Tallawampa was just too isolated for them to be reached. Bombs burst over the South but Tallawampa's recesses gave it immunity. That was the prudent and reasoned conviction. But then one day over Route 24 came Wardel Mackel, and all heads raised and all eyes opened as a stillness fell over Tallawampa.

Chapter Two

The exact date that Wardel came to Tallawampa is not known and later the local citizens speculated as to whom had seen him first. But whoever it was and whatever the date, it was some time in early March. Wardel was physically slight but muscular and had a prominent roundness of his deltoid muscles. His face was flat and rectangular with wide piercing eyes that you could look into separately. His skin was an unusual darkness, not colored like the local negroes but almost a slate blackness; this particular darkness made him very visible wherever he went. His walk was also different from the local negroes, being directional and with purpose rather than ambling and migratory. It was rumored he was from Michigan; that he was involved with the students at Tuskegee as well as with other civil rights groups. But wherever he was from little was known about his background. If the local citizens could have looked into past tenements and ghettos where he was spawned, they would have seen a small dark fatherless child raised in deprivation on starch often shared with varmin, struggling and somewhat bewildered by his placement in time and space, slowly developing the awareness of the inequities placed on him. Later they would have seen him gradually absorbing weights and burdens, provoked by taunts, ridicule, and indifference to his insignificance. But if these weights deprived joy from Wardel's life, they gave him strength; and his lonely isolation and exclusion tempered in him a determination that was rooted in his bones. Wardel was not oblivious to the dangers that awaited him in Tallawampa or for that matter, any other community that he com-

18

mitted himself to. For Wardel the civil rights movement was more than a swelling tide to refresh dampened psychological impulses; it was an instrument for change.

In the beginning Wardel came with companions, other colored youngsters, mostly boys but occasionally girls, and rarely a white. Later he came more and more often alone. He first visited the colored churches and spoke with their ministers. These men were receptive to him but they had reservations and they extended a guarded hospitality to the new interloper. Other colored groups in town were also receptive but they equally had reservations and moved with guarded hospitality. All these persons were somewhat suspicious for they dreaded the bombs that were exploding across Dixie as much as anyone else. He was given permission to address the congregations of the churches; one of the congregations he addressed was Mount Zion. On all these occasions his calls were for action and his homilies had tones of retribution and hints of ultimatums. His suggestions of provocative acts aroused fears in his audiences. "That might be fine for you young man but what are we going to do after you leave? We have to stay here and live with these people." When his messages failed to elicit the activity he wanted, he continued with greater determination and force that only increased the timidity of his audiences.

His calls for direct action also caused confusion. They should defy the edicts placed upon them, break laws, and do things illegal. He organized demonstrations to use the segregated bathrooms and drinking fountains at the courthouse, a well as campaign for citizens to register to vote. But at the stated time for these acts, only he and his out-of-town friends appeared for the demonstrations. The day for the voter registration the halls of the courthouse remained deserted. Wardel and friends used the water fountain and the lavatory; they sat outside the registrar's office which remained closed all day. Not a single person passed them on that Monday. During their vigil Sheriff Redtop spent the day in his office not more than one hundred feet away waiting for a spark to set him in motion. Others watched from windows of various buildings around courthouse square, awestruck, waiting for an explosion. That night the courthouse door was left unlocked and by morning Wardel and his friends were gone. There were sighs of relief, and the next day he wasn't seen, nor the next after that. And then on the third day, "He's gone! He's left!" "Are you sure?" But several days later he was back.

Again Wardel was granted the privilege to address the congregations of the churches. But this time his calls for corrective actions had more vehemence than before and less conciliation than ever. There was now more defiance and stronger ultimatums that caused even greater apprehensions. These returns to the pulpits caused such alarm that he was denied access to this forum again. But he continued his courting of these congregations and his interruptions of the services now caused only embarrassment. Yet Wardel could not be turned away; he continued to attend and socialize, always cajoling them to activity with messages of freedom through voter registration. The timidity that he provoked was now extending into mistrust.

One Saturday when Tallawampa was full of buyers and people transacting business, Wardel went to Mellon's. He sat down at one of the tables in full view of First Street. No one else was sitting at the tables when Wardel appeared and the only two people at the counter quickly left when he entered the restaurant. The Mellons stayed in the kitchen, struck with fear. He asked to see a menu and was told by the waitress, "We only have sandwiches today."

"I'll have a ham sandwich." When she returned with the sandwich Wardel looked at her white hands without raising his head to look at her face. "May I have a glass of water," he said with force. The girl returned in silence with the glass. He ate alone in Mellon's and not a single person passed on First Street the whole time he was there. He was not presented with a check and after eating finally placed a dollar on the table and left. The incident was noted by all but commented on by none.

The following Saturday Tallawampa was again packed with the county's residents; this time Wardel appeared on the courthouse steps at high noon. "Listen everyone, listen to me, we're going to integrate and have freedom now!" People about the square turned in disbelief as he continued. "We shall throw down our shackles!" He continued in the hot sun with sweat pouring off his face as he called out cries for civil disobedience.

It wasn't really a crowd that had collected to listen to him but rather the people who were already there when he began to speak. Their reactions were a mixture of disbelief, hostility, confusion and doubt. "That ain't the way to do it boy," thought some. But those present melted away and before long the only people left were

20

Sheriff Redtop with his deputies, leaning on the fenders of their cars, booted, badged, hatted and holstered, peering from behind tinted glasses.

In the crowd that day at the courthouse there were two other men, both new to Tallawampa. They were quiet, clean shaven, polite, salesmen, one insurance and the other lumber supplies. They were never together; each made his rounds of Tallawampa, going to all the local establishments; they didn't seem to sell either of their products and it didn't seem to matter to them. They bought items at the various stores, used the barber shop, ate at Mellon's and even went to the Route 24 eatery. Both of these men had gone to the courthouse several times, one to get various licenses while the other made inquiries about recorded deeds and plats of land. These men watched Wardel's delivery that day, one from his car, the other from Prichard's store, silent, curious, detached, almost investigative.

After Wardel's address at the courthouse the attendance of his companions became progressively sporadic and less frequent. Some time later it was noted that Wardel was in Tallawampa in the mornings before the bus arrived. He was staying overnight. On occasions there was a car parked by his room near the train tracks. Twice Redtop on his own searched Wardel's quarters while the room was empty. There was but a single mattress on the floor, a few cans of soup and a hot plate, crackers and an empty carton of milk. There were also a few books and pieces of literature placed haphazardly around the room. There was not a single chair or bureau and no toilet facilities.

Wardel's residence in Tallawampa increased the concern and watchfulness by the local people. Judge Newbold saw Wardel only once and that was from the window of the courthouse, but he watched and followed his activities with concern and calculated the possible courses of actions that might become necessary. John Prichard watched Wardel as well, and he though about other possibilities—supposing John would have to prosecute Wardel; or what was worse, if something happened to Wardel, then what would John have to do. There was another group that watched Wardel—those who lived nearer to him in the same part of town. Their concerns were not the same as the Judge's or prosecutor's. They sat in dark hidden places glaring from concealed perches looking for weaknesses. They began with distant threats, gradually becoming

21

bolder, hollering racial vulgarities from passing cars. When these same people identified Wardel's car, they cut the tires and broke the windshield. Finally they painted the engine of the car with tar. One evening they broke the windows in his room and on another they broke in, painting the walls with obscenities. Ross Brooks was the captain of this group of ruffians that considered themselves an honor guard to society's rules for existing structure. Ross was the fountainhead of this local council and this swelled him with pride.

Ross had been born in Birmingham and he and his mother's excursions had taken them as far as Chattanooga; like others, he was a composite of his genes and his environment; like Wardel, he was conceived unknown, born unrecognized and fatherless. It was this latter trait, the fatherlessness, that would prove to be disastrous for Ross as it would also be for Wardel. From his earliest years Ross had been exposed to sights and sounds no child should witness; mistreated by numerous of his mother's paramours, he would carry those scars for life. The slurs of those contemptuous companions drove deep into Ross a lack of esteem and self worth—"You're a nasty little bastard, aren't you"—such expletives had long ceased and though faded, their accumulative weight had marked his personality forever.

When he matured Ross was heavy, slow, broadly built and cumbersome. If he lacked grace, there was nevertheless strength in Ross. There was also a central core of hostility, and suspicion existed just beneath his surface that was easily aroused. These two traits, hostility and suspicion, had been engraved into Ross by the same maternal suitors as Ross and his mother had travelled across the deep south in itinerant fashion during his formative years. There had been only transient friendships and transient schools and soon he was isolated in the crowd at the very edge of society. He left home and school during the eighth grade; he was just 16. He pursued various jobs as an unskilled and semi-skilled labor, indoors as a scullion and outdoors in refuse and service work. He was more comfortable at the latter and finally acquired sufficient service skills that gave him access to other manual jobs.

There were callous efforts to establish manhood that had failed. There had been only one serious problem with the law for which he had spent fourteen months in the Tennessee State Penitentiary, this for auto theft. After that he had drifted slowly across Alabama again picking up odd jobs and seeing occasional friends in Birmingham and Bessemer. There he took up residence and lived with a coterie of hollow friends in medium vulgarity.

But if this collection of people had streaks of meanness in them produced by abuse or by neglect from past relationships, to their credit they stayed to themselves and seldom wandered where they were unfamiliar or unwanted. They spent nights in dull intoxication, innoculated other members with contagion and defended an imaginary cult. This cult was a burning issue to them and they were reassured through public signs everywhere of the established order and of their rightful position in society. By birth Ross and his friends were superior and by birth they could never be equalled.

In Ross' gradual ascent he finally obtained a job with the railroad. For the railroad he had worked in Montgomery, strange to him, beautiful and peaceful. It was the railroad that brought Ross further south to Tallawampa; he liked the town as he had liked Montgomery. It too was peaceful and beautiful. Working for the railroad he established residence in Tallawampa in its industrial community adjacent to the railroad tracks.

But even here in the security of this isolated community there were now intrusions to alter the established order. The civil rights events of the past several years had been welcomed by Ross and his friends; it gave an opportunity for what they considered their side to exert control, as well as reaffirm and demonstrate their superiority. They followed the social events with pride and resolve. It renewed their confidence in their supremacy and also provoked acts of contempt on some of the local citizens who they considered to be of lesser stature. With the news of each new bombing and explosion there were cries of vindication. But those events were far away and now Wardel Mackel changed all of this. Mackel was here in their midst, not some son-of-a-bitch a hundred miles away carrying a sign, but right here in Tallawampa. What was worse, Wardel didn't even acknowledge them. It was to Mellons that Wardel had gone, not to the diner by the railroad tracks; it was to the courthouse he had gone and to the churches; places even they didn't go. Wardel had called a meeting and he had given a speech on the courthouse steps. Ross and his friends spent their days in perplexity about Wardel's activities and their nights with cans of Falstaff and pinballs, drawing up vague battle plans with calls for action. Each new council brought greater

23

demands for boldness. After they had ruined Wardel's car, there were many episodes of obscenities screamed from speeding cars; they finally confronted Wardel one night in front of his room. There were four of them, each saturated with booze. They encircled Wardel, punching at him, slapped him on the head, and pushed him into the wall. They spewed out violent remarks, but Wardel just stood there looking at one and then another; he didn't even speak.

"I'm talking to you, you black son-of-a-bitch." They pushed him into the wall again. Their voices raised as they encircled their captive. The four of them moved in disjointed directions, flailing their arms, glancing at each other to gather their strength, Wardel standing there still, not moving. One of the four then suddenly bolted towards their car. Soon they were speeding away to roars of satisfaction leaving Wardel standing as he had been before the altercation.

By the middle of April, the preoccupation by all the citizens of Tallawampa with Wardel's activities became less. Most people turned their attention to outings and picnics. There were preparations necessary for the Confederate Memorial Day Parade and this year the planning committee was even considering having chairs for the colored band from Booker T. Washington High School at the reviewing stands before the courthouse; after the Memorial Day activities, there would be the graduations with new dresses, suits, parties and dances. All of Tallawampa, including John and Jenny, sank into a welcomed shift of pace with greater emphasis on leisure and lightness.

The last weekend in May John and Jenny had driven to Grove Hill to visit her family—her parents, two sisters and one brother-in-law. Jenny's younger sister liked John while the older (and married) sister did not. John thought that this was so because Laura (the younger sister) liked Jenny and since John was Jenny's husband, therefore, she liked John, while Sharon (the older sister) who doesn't like Jenny, therefore, didn't like John. John had put these relationships into an algebraic equation that looked something like the following: Laura likes Jenny because Sharon doesn't like Jenny; Sharon doesn't like Jenny because Jenny is nicer than Sharon. Therefore, Laura doesn't like Sharon because Sharon is the oldest, self-centered and often a pain in the neck; the square root of all this was Jenny liked Laura, is nice to Sharon and really didn't give a hoot or a holler otherwise.

There had been much talk that day about the new changes that

24

this year was bringing and the blame for all of the turmoil was clearly laid at the proper feet. This list of changes for the turmoil were drawn up chiefly by Jenny's dad with Sharon giving her valuable insights and the subservient support of the brother-in-law. When John and Jenny returned to Tallawampa that evening, their conversation was about the people of Grove Hill and Jenny's family. She analyzed the changes in her family and friends, reflected on insights into personalities that only time and distance can bring. They were pleasant reflections. Throughout the trip home as they moved along Route 24, John's thoughts wandered between Jenny's analyses of her family and Wardel. The attacks on Wardel had become more brazen and aggressive. Perhaps with the slower pace of summer there would be no explosion. All this would pass, but the aura and premonition of disaster continued throughout the remainder of the day and into the evening. When they reached their home, a soothing stillness erased John's apprehensions. It was a sweet, cool evening spent with favors and gifts and on the morning the stillness continued as did the perfumed delights. A breeze began the outside world and John turned to coffee and paper to begin renewed and refreshed. At nine o'clock the phone rang.

"Mr. Prichard, this is Jack Hawes," the voice began hurried and excited. "Sheriff Redtop asked me to call you. They found Mackel dead this morning, in a ditch, been shot! It must have happened some time last night." There was a pause as Hawes waited for John to react to the news. "Are you there, are you there, Mr. Prichard?"

"Yes, I'm here," said John. "Who found him?" John added.

"Two F.B.I. agents!" responded Hawes.

"F.B.I. agents! What two F.B.I. agents?"

"Those two salesmen that have been in town, one of them sells lumber and I don't know what the other one sells but it doesn't make any difference anyway, cause neither one of them are salesmen. They're F.B.I. agents—they found him." Hawes continued, "Out by Mount Zion field, he was in the woods just off the ball field shot in the back and in the head. How those two F.B.I. agents knew about Mount Zion field I don't know, but they did."

"Have you seen the body yet?"

"Yes, sir. I saw it out there, face down. It's still out there, too," answered Hawes.

"Where's the Sheriff?"

"He's out there with the body," continued Hawes. "He and Lester are out there."

"How about the two F.B.I. agents?" asked John.

"They're out there, too."

"You mean the Sheriff and Lester and the two F.B.I. agents are out there?" asked John.

"That's right, that's right."

"Shot, you say, in the back and in the head." John continued, "Is there anyone besides me, you, the Sheriff and Lester and the F.B.I. agents who know about this?"

"Not that I know of," responded Hawes. "We haven't told anyone. The two agents called the Sheriff this morning at about six o'clock and told him that they had found Mackel dead. One of them met the Sheriff over at his house. I don't know how those fellas knew that Mackel was dead but they called the Sheriff and the one went to the Sheriff's house. The Sheriff called me and Lester. The other agent must have stayed out at Mount Zion with the body. That's all I know about it and the four of them are still out there."

"Have the F.B.I. agents talked to anyone besides the Sheriff?" asked John.

"Not that I know of."

"Where are you now, Jack?"

"At the jail by myself." That was the first time Hawes' voice displayed seriousness instead of excitement.

"Jack, call the Sheriff and tell him I'll be out there as soon as I can get dressed. I'll bring the coroner with me and don't talk to anyone about this. Call Langford (the coroner) and tell him there's been an accident and I'll be by to pick him up in fifteen minutes. Don't give him any details of the event."

After John's conversation with Deputy Hawes, he dialed the seven exchange, a local number that is located west of town toward the river. After several rings Judge Thomas Newbold answered. "Judge, this is John Prichard. How are you this morning."

"Fine," the Judge responded. "What can I do for you, John?"

"Judge, I have some bad news, some very bad news. I just had a call from Deputy Jack Hawes who told me that Wardel Mackel has been shot and killed. They found him out by Mount Zion field back in the woods. He's been shot in the head and through the back. He was found by the two salesmen who've been in and out of town recently;

26

they are apparently F.B.I. agents. Redtop and Lester are out there still with the agents. I thought I'd call Langford and we'd drive out there right away to see what we can find out. Is there anything that you want me to do?"

There was a silence from the other end of the line; finally Thomas Newbold responded, "No, no. I don't think so, John." There was another pause and then the Judge continued, "Seems regrettable, doesn't it. I suppose a lot of us were worried that something like this would happen." When the Judge did not continue John concluded, "I'll keep you informed, Judge."

"Fine, John, fine."

Jenny was awake now because of the telephone conversations and as John dressed she began, "I couldn't help but hear the conversation, is there anything—"

"There's been an accident, nobody we know though."

"Serious?" asked Jenny.

John nodded as he continued to dress.

"Someone shot that colored boy?" asked Jenny.

John nodded again. Jenny walked to the window and looked out the curtain at her garden and parts of Semmes Street. "He's dead?" she asked. "Murdered? What will happen?" she asked.

"I don't know," said John turning as he was putting on the last of his informal wardrobe. "I don't know," he repeated.

"What will happen if it is murder?" she asked.

He stood still for a moment and continued. "I don't know that either. If it's murder and you have evidence and a suspect, I guess you have to prosecute that person, and since I'm the prosecutor I guess that would be my job." He reflected on his comments and then went on. "I've never tried a racial murder before but if there's been a murder, you just can't pretend it didn't happen, so I guess if there's evidence and a suspect and I'm the prosecuting attorney, I'll have to prosecute someone. Maybe it was an accident," he added. "We'll have to wait and find out what happened. Honey, call Langford and tell him I'll be by to pick him up and that it's very serious."

"Do you want breakfast before you go? Coffee?"

"No, I'm fine," John replied. "I've had some coffee."

It's only a twenty-minute drive from Tallawampa to Mount Zion field. John picked up the coroner Warren Langford, and the two men then drove toward Mount Zion. It was a beautiful day, the mo

27

ning still cool with calm and peacefulness. It couldn't have been a better or nicer time to have been alive. John had driven down this road a thousand times at least; he had hunted here and hunted there. He knew every farm and every house. There was the turn for the road that went to Franklin's house. Franklin had been a member of the Mount Zion Church and had served as one of its elders. He had worked for John's father as long as John could remember, stable and dependable. John recalled his father and Franklin in busy activity with customers during Saturdays and the two of them sitting in the store alone during slack times, each at his station in uneven symbiosis. It had been dad's store that brought John to where he was. Dad, who had never missed a day in all those years, had never taken a vacation, always had every item stocked for every customer. Selling briskly some days or waiting at long intervals for someone to come in and buy a bag of nails, going over ledgers and inventories, thoroughness and discipline. It had been Dad who had provided the means and direction for John to go to law school. And Franklin, almost like a surrogate father, equally dependable and responsible, setting example. Franklin had been John's friend, someone older, someone to emulate. Franklin must have been John's father's friend as well for those two men to have worked together for so long. Yet as close as those two men had been there was little verbal communication between them. It was rare for Franklin to have been mentioned at home, and he had never come to the house. The only contact occurred at the store. Franklin, with his wife and daughter, Cora, came to the store periodically. These visits were semi-business and semi-social. In all those years the Prichards had the store John had gone to Franklin's house only once. It was on a winter's night and John with his father had driven out to Franklin's to deliver a check. When they went inside, the house was dimly lighted and smelled of kerosene oil. The room was small and decorated with faded unmatched paints. It was barely large enough to contain its five occupants. The ceiling was low and the floor was tilted. A curtain divided the front room from a back room. Behind the curtain you could see a portion of a sink and table—a kitchen. This visit was a discovery for John. His mind wondered at the surroundings. "This is how they live." The room, though small and worn, was clean and neat. In one corner there was a chair and some books on a shelf. Perhaps a dozen texts, probably school books he thought, a regular carrel here at Franklin's.

"They read! My, God!" The adults exchanged pleasantries that evening and joked; there were inquiries about Cora's progress in school. She blushed through her dark skin; Cora was probably two years older than John, maybe sixteen. She was excited by their visit; she beamed, she smiled and moved her hands and head in all directions—company right here in her house, Mr. Prichard and John. They stayed but a few moments and didn't even sit. John Sr. gave Franklin the check. What a brief exchange for someone you had known so long.

Franklin had died while John was away at college and he had missed the funeral. But Franklin's passing did not dissolve his family, and Cora continued Bama State to obtain her teaching certificate. After graduation she taught for a few years in the local schools and then migrated to some place in Illinois. She returned summers to visit her aging widowed mother. As the years passed the visits became less frequent, and when Cora's mother finally passed away she returned for the last time. She was young, perhaps thirty-five, but tired, weary and discouraged. The burial of her mother closed Cora's childhood and ended her life in Tallawampa. John's thoughts hovered on Franklin and Franklin's family as he and the coroner continued their drive to Mount Zion field. How close the Prichards and Days had been for all those years but how far apart. As they approached nearer to Mount Zion field, John told the coroner the events of the previous night as had been told to him by the Sheriff's deputy. John did not include his conversation with the Judge. The two men drove down Tangent Road that was still moist with dew so that the car raised no dust. At the backstop there were two cars, the Sheriff's and a Chevrolet evidently used by the agents. Lester was sitting in the Sheriff's car waiting for John and the coroner to arrive. When the deputy saw the men approaching, he stepped from his car and approached the prosecutor and coroner. "We have him alright, dead as a door nail. Blew a hole in his head big enough to put your fist in. The Sheriff's back there now watching the body with those two guys." John, with the other two, began walking through the infield toward Loggen Road through the thick grass that had been matted down by the wheels of a car. "Walk to the right on the path, out there, there are some footprints and blood we might want to save," cautioned Lester as they walked on. At the edge of the field and the woods, Loggen Road continued into the forest This road is

29

slightly elevated above the adjoining terrain of scrub pine, the pines next to Loggen Road having been bush hogged. Redtop and the two agents were less than sixty feet down the road. Sure enough, it was the two salesmen, Crowley and Leonard. As John approached the three he could see someone lying in the grass on the road, face down, covered by a blanket, his right hand and two feet extending beyond the margins of the covering. Redtop was obviously pleased to see friends with whom he felt more at ease. Everyone exchanged pleasantries; there was a genteel formality that surprised John as he watched Redtop and his deputy perform polite cordialities. Everyone shook hands, Mr. this and Mr. that, just like the tossing of a coin at a football game—well met, hail and hardy. The graciousness of it as the sextet stood there. There was a pause to see who would take the initiative. Then John began to speak.

"Wardel Mackel?" John asked looking at the men and then down at the blanket. They all nodded in agreement. John stooped and pulled the blanket gently back from the head and looked at the bullet wound. The face was distorted but still recognizable. "Wardel Mackel, all right. No question about that." All nodded again in the affirmative

"I know him," continued Redtop. "I have fingerprints on him too, and we can take them from the body as well."

"Do we know what happened?" asked John. The other men looked at each other for a few moments and then at Crowley, one of the F.B.I. agents.

Crowley began, "The Mount Zion Church had its picnic yesterday evening. I understand it's an annual event for the church, with chicken, soft drinks, ice tea, games, no alcohol; Wardel Mackel was one of the guests or at least one of those here. No trouble and everything went fine; a subdued pleasant church gathering. When it started to get dusk or dark, the picnic began to break up. About that time some of the members of the church noticed a car, '52 Ford, that needed body work with a some whites in it, three or four of them, depending on which person you listen to. It's not quite sure what happened as people were leaving, whether the presence of the car caused them to leave or whether they were just leaving on their own, I'm not sure either; but in any event they gathered their things and left. Wardel's presence seems to have been lost during that time. Then early this morning we were called and told that Wardel hadn't

30

been seen since the picnic. We went by his room and he hadn't re-
turned. We then drove out here and found things as they are now.
No cars were here but there was evidence of the picnic and there
were marks in the field where a car had been driven to the edge of
the outfield and this road. The car didn't come down here but there
were a number of footprints. You can see down there," Crowley
pointed toward the field, "where the car turned around and drove
away through the infield. It drove through the backstop tearing
through the wire and uprooting the poles. You probably saw the
footprints on the path as you walked down here." By now Crowley
had started walking back toward right field as he continued his narra-
tive. Pointing, he added, "there are two sets of footprints, one has a
longer stride and must have been Mackel's running down the road.
Also there are a few drops of blood by some of these sets of foot-
prints. The other set of footprints are of a shorter stride and must
have been made by a shorter person or someone who was not in as
much of a hurry. Mackel collapsed here and that's where we found
him. We found two bullet casings by the body and four near where
the car turned at the edge of the field."

Silence followed when Crowley finished his narrative. "Do we
know who did it?" asked John. There was still silence and when no
one answered John continued, "Do we know anybody who has a
'52 black Ford that needs body work and that has recently been
driven through a backstop made of chickenwire?"

"We can find out whose car it is, I think," said the Sheriff.

"Do we have any suspects," asked John. There was again
silence and the two agents looked at Redtop and Lester. Lester kept
his eyes down and Warren Langford, standing next to him, visibly
perspired.

Redtop began, "One of those fellows who lives over by the rail-
road, in fact Ross Brooks, apparently was doing some bragging late
last night, but of course there is no proof, saying how he took care of
this fellow and said he shot him. I guess if you can take that as true,
not just bragging, I suppose he's a suspect."

"Who was he bragging to?" inquired John.

"A group of them were over at that drinking place on Route 24
late last night, you know the crowd, young kids, and Brooks was tell-
ing people in there what they had done. I had a call after midnight
telling me that they were bragging about what had allegedly hap-

31

pened. Brooks told everybody how the four of them came out here and roughed up Mackel, then when he started talking back, how they weren't going to take any smart talk from no common goddamn nigger, they started shoving him around. There was a fracas and Brooks shot him." The Sheriff hesitated and again began nervously. "It being dark and everything, I didn't see any sense in coming out here last night. I thought I'd come out here this morning and when I was getting ready to come out I had a phone call from Mr. Crowley here. That's all I know and that's all I've heard," concluded Redtop relieved by his confession.

"Is the car his?" asked John. Redtop shook his head yes. "I suppose you better arrest Ross Brooks and put him in jail at least for the time being," continued John. "Do you know who were the others with Brooks in the car?" asked John.

"No, but I'm sure I can find out," replied the Sheriff.

"Unless there are no objections, Warren," John said turning to Langford, the coroner, "pick up the body and take it back to Tallawampa. Hold it there and maybe we'll want to do an autopsy."

Langford's mouth dropped. "An autopsy," he asked in shock. "Why would we want to do an autopsy; we've never done an autopsy. This boy's been shot anyway; why, we know what killed him."

"Well, we might want one."

But Langford continued, "We've never had an autopsy; I just don't," he sputtered for a few moments and then stopped, looking at John. "Well, if that's what you think, we'll certainly hold the body until you tell me what to do. You let me know what to do, yes, sir. I'll make arrangements right now." Langford walked down the road toward the cars.

John left Langford with Lester and returned to home alone. It had finally happened, Tallawampa's racial murder. He wasn't surprised, everyone had been watching for something like this; and some had been waiting for it. Somehow that which was never going to happen, did, and it happened right here in Tallawampa. John wasn't sure what to do, but there were eight people who knew about the murder already, and with Jenny that made nine. Two of those who knew were F.B.I. agents, one was a sheriff, another a judge and one a prosecutor. Redtop had already been instructed to arrest Ross Brooks; that was his job and he would do it. There was nothing to do but prosecute; there was enough evidence already and within a few minutes a suspect would be arrested. It hadn't been two hours since the deputy had called John at home about the murder. How quickly things happen. John was sure that this news would be disseminated rapidly. No telling how many people were in that bar last night with Brooks doing his bragging and today everyone in town would know what happened. There apparently were three witnesses to the shooting and identifying them ought to be easy. There must be a gun somewhere if Mackel was shot; it would be the Sheriff's business to find that. It seemed like an obvious murder for an obvious reason and the outcome was also equally obvious. The case was open and shut. A trouble maker in town agitating everybody, being provocative, and shot by a roughneck.

To prosecute someone for shooting Wardel Mackel was one thing, that was the easy part, and John knew it; but to convict someone of the same crime would be impossible and John knew that too. He drove along, analyzing the events. Why would it be impossible he asked himself? No question what happened; no question that it was murder; why should this fellow get away with what he did. Wardel Mackel was no peach but he wasn't a jackrabbit either. Maybe we could do it, John thought to himself. Maybe we could get him convicted. John wasn't sure which one of the local toughs Ross Brooks was but he was bound to have more friends than Wardel Mackel. Wardel wasn't liked in town—he was probably more of an annoyance than anything for many people; and Brooks had not been in trouble locally which meant if you pitted those two against each other in a trial Brooks would win that contest—at least here in Alabama he would. No way a jury of twelve locals would pick Wardel over Brooks. There must be some way to get him convicted, though. Judge Newbold would give me a fair trial, he would let the chips fall as they may. The jury—that would be the key, thought John. How could I get twelve people to convict Ross Brooks for what he did. They would never do it, he thought. Maybe half of them would, but to get twelve out of twelve, there would always be a couple who wouldn't stand for it. That would be the problem, the selection of the jury. With the selection of the jury maybe I could get it down to a few—he interrupted his thought—it's not the selection of the jury, he continued, what I would have to do is get the jury to identify with me rather than with Ross Brooks. It has to be a contest between Ross Brooks and me, John Prichard, not Ross Brooks and Wardel

33

Mackel. That's the way and it shouldn't be too difficult to do. Nobody in Alabama had ever convicted a white of killing a black, and if I can do that, it would be a first. The only way to do it is to beat Ross Brooks one on one. Make the jury pick between me or Ross Brooks. John drove along and he wasn't even back to town yet.

John continued his thoughts. There will be lots of publicity. I wonder what all of them will think; the Judge hadn't said much on the phone when John had told him about the murder. And the Judge as well as the town would not want all of the publicity the murder would bring, but there was no way to avoid that. John's thoughts continued with the Judge. Thomas Newbold was no coward, no problem there. What will the town think about the prosecution, John went on to himself. The autopsy came to John's mind. That's it, he reassured himself; I'll ask Langford to do the autopsy and I'll ask Dr. Christy to be there, and if Doc Christy says yes, I'm on the right track, and if he says no, then there's no hope. He drove on toward home and his thoughts returned to Jenny.

By early afternoon the phone had begun to ring. All the calls were for Jenny, people telling her of the circumstances of the previous night. "Really," she would reply. "Why he doesn't tell me a thing." Local people by the score and local phone calls by the hundreds crisscrossed Tallawampa telling all the events of the previous night. There was even a call from Grove Hill, Jenny's dad. By midafternoon Redtop came to the house. He parked out front facing in the wrong direction. John went outside and met him on the walkway.

"Well, I have him locked up, Mr. Prosecutor," Redtop stated. "I tried to call you but your line was busy. I have spoken with the Highway Patrol and I told them that we could handle it. I told them we had made an arrest already."

"Did Brooks offer any trouble?" asked John.

"No," responded Redtop with authority, "but I put the handcuffs on him anyway just to let him know," Redtop added with emphasis. "We went by his room this morning after we left the field and he was still sleeping. We woke him up and told him what the charges were. I told him to come along peacefully and to cooperate with us and it would be a lot better for him. Brooks didn't admit anything or deny it either but kind of alluded to the thing, half bragging, sometimes serious and sometimes joking." Redtop, knowing that John

34

didn't want to talk to the prisoner, looked at John and asked, "Do you want to talk to him?"

"No, I don't believe so," responded John. "Not just yet anyway."

Redtop then informed John that Langford had called him and wanted to know about the autopsy and what he should do about the body. Langford had had the body delivered to the only black undertaker in town, one Amos Rumph. There was no way that Langford could have desecrated his white mortuary table with the remains of Wardel. What was worse for the coroner was that if there was to be an autopsy, he would have to go to the black funeral home to do it. Langford had already decided that if the autopsy was necessary rather than use Rumph's instruments he would use his own. To do this he would have to swear Rumph to secrecy, enforceable by threats and intimidations of loss of his license if he dared tell anyone. Rumph would keep his mouth shut. John assured the Sheriff that he would call the coroner to tell him what arrangements had been made and he would take care of that presently.

John returned into the house and called Dr. Christy who was the only physician in town. In fact, he was the only physician in the county, who was now approaching his seventy-third year. He had delivered everyone, treated everyone, patched everyone and purged everyone. Doc Christy's office was one of the wonders of Tallawampa. He had office hours in the mornings, afternoons and evenings, five days a week, Monday through Friday. Since nearly everyone in the county worked at something, it was the evening hours that were the busiest. During the winter months in the flu season and on Monday nights, in particular, which was a catch-up night, there would be more people in that single waiting room than there would have been at the various Sunday services the day before. Each patient registered with the nurse and took a number. Black abscesses, white boils, black and white angina, ring worms, sugar diabetes, swollen ankles, runny noses, double pneumonia, each in their turn or need. If Jesus came into Dr. Christy's office on one of those Monday nights with an ingrown toenail, the best he could hope for would be to be squeezed between the sugar diabetes and the runny noses. For those who didn't like mixed proceedings or were offended by these democratic ways, they could come during the day; mornings reserved for one group and the afternoons for the other.

35

Dr. Chirsty was a quiet, pleasant man with an oval friendly face and a pleasing disposition.

Now in midafternoon events of the previous evening shooting had been sufficiently spread that John was certain that the doctor knew of the murder. "Doctor, this is John Prichard. I suppose you've heard about the misfortune we've had here in town. That fellow, Wardel Mackel, was shot and killed."

"Yes, I heard," the doctor responded.

"Doctor, he was shot several times and Warren Langford has held the body. I'm not quite sure of the events of the shooting and wondered if an autopsy would be useful."

"Well, I don't do autopsies, John," responded the physician.

"I didn't mean for you to do the autopsy yourself, doctor. I thought we'd let Warren do that, but if you could be there and look at the wounds to see what you thought of them that maybe that would be helpful."

There was a silence and the doctor responded, "I suppose I could do that, I'm not sure that you need any help from me but I could look and see what I thought."

"Thank you, doctor," responded John, surprised by his own enthusiasm. "I'll call Warren and let you know what the arrangements are."

"Fine," responded the doctor. He thanked John for the phone call and hung up the receiver. Jenny had been in the kitchen during the telephone conversation and inquired to whom John was speaking. When John responded, "nobody," she didn't comment on not being included.

"I'm going to walk over to Langford's, Jenny," and she watched John leave the house and walk toward Langford's.

Langford's is a semi-large house well known for its well-kept lawn and its bright green shutters. Awnings covered the windows in the summer months and added what Warren Langford considered a dignified look. There is a side entrance to Langford's and John thought he would use this since he was on business, the front door being reserved for family and friends who came there to mourn. However, when he reached Langford's he went to the front door anyway. Langford answered the door himself in his shirtsleeves, chewing on what was obviously a part of his lunch. He looked disappointed when he saw John and was sure that John's suggestion for an autopsy was not only an imposition but a source of trouble. "Has anyone claimed the body yet?" began John.

"Two of the colored ministers have called and said that they would take him. I told them that it wasn't ready to be released and for them to call back." Langford was returning toward his kitchen as he answered the question. John followed and informed Langford that he had spoken with Dr. Christy and that the two of them felt it was important to examine the body. Langford stood there without answering but with a look upon his face—I suppose you want to do this now and interrupt my lunch; John, anticipating his unasked question, looked back with a positive gaze that meant yes, that's exactly what I want.

"I suppose you'll want the Sheriff there as well?" asked Langford.

"No, I don't believe so," responded John. "Dr. Christy, you and myself should be enough. There's no reason to bother the Sheriff."

"Well, I guess we can get started. It's curious that we should examine a body like this; we've never done it before. In all my years as coroner I've never done an autopsy. Are you anticipating any touble or any problems?"

"No," John responded, "I don't anticipate any problems but we want to do what's right."

"Well, of course, we want to do what's right," answered Langford. Since he was shot in the back, I guess you'll want to have him face down to examine the body? I suppose we'll have to go through the back to examine him."

"We might have to look at both sides," responded John. "I'll call Dr. Christy. Should I tell him to meet us in an hour at Rumph's? How about five o'clock?" The two of them agreed upon the time and John left to inform Dr. Christy. When John reached home, he phoned the physician and told him of their rendezvous at Rumph's at the appointed time. Afterwards, John went about the house; he examined the Time magazine on the coffee table. It sat in front of the TV set across the room, a nineteen-inch screen, very dark like a big mouth with two dials for eyes. He thumbed through the magazine and the TV guide. All of these articles, all of these shows, each with a message, plain, obvious or subtle. Someone sitting at a large desk miles away wanting to distribute this or that piece of information, to tell this or that story, to submit this to the editor, to make this addition or

37

deletion. The presentations so polished and persuasive. New art, new literature he thought. He watched the clock anticipating his five o'clock meeting; he ate a sandwich and drank a glass of milk. He walked from room to room about the house touching talismans. "Jenny, I'm going out for a while." It was only four-thirty but he was anxious to get started. She smiled without responding and John went to the black undertaker's.

When he reached Rumph's, both Warren and the doctor were already there and had started. Amos Rumph had been instructed by Warren to wait outside on the stoop of his own funeral home; he was also told that he would be called when the autopsy was completed. Wardel had been placed on the embalming table face down. There were three bullet wounds—one to the back of the head, one to the chest to the left of the midline, and one to the inner aspect of the left upper thigh. "The shot to the head must have killed him," said John.

"You would think so, but that's an awful large bullet hole through bone," the doctor added. "Look at the inside of the leg, Warren, and see if you can locate a bullet," the doctor said turning to the mortician.

Warren did as he was asked. He palpated the inner surface of the thigh with his fingers for a moment. "Here it is! I have it!" he said. The doctor instructed Langford to cut the skin of the leg over the bullet and after he had done so the bullet dropped out.

"So that bullet struck him in the back of the leg and ended up in the subcutaneous tissue of the front of the thigh. The leg's not swollen so it must not have hit a significant vessel. Warren, open up the leg from where the bullet went in to where it stopped under the skin."

Warren obeyed. He opened the tract of the bullet wound throughout its length. "There is only a small amount of hemorrhage so it didn't hit a significant artery throughout its trail," repeated the doctor. John and Warren looked at each other trying to determine the significance of the doctor's statement. "Let's look at that head for a moment." Dr. Christy moved to the head of the table. "That's a big wound with multiple fragments of bone. I suppose they're all there. But there's no hemorrhage and the brain's just torn into pieces." The doctor pursed his lips, pondering his next step; John and Warren looked at each other again, unsure of the significance of the doctor's statements. "Warren, you'll have to clean that out and save any bullet fragments that you find for John. We should open the body and see what that bullet to the chest did and where it went." John wasn't sure what this information would lead to but agreed. Both John and the doctor stook back and looked at Warren.

"I'll turn him over," Warren said without question. The other two men stepped back from the table while Warren turned the body over. It was twenty minutes before Warren had the chest open and when he removed the breast plate there was a bullet stuck to its inner surface. Inside the chest the left pleural cavity and mediastinum (the space in the chest between the two lung cavities) were filled with blood. The bullet had entered the back and lacerated the superior surface of the common pulmonary artery at its bifurcation into its right and left branches. From there the bullet lodged into the posterior aspect of the sternum or breast bone. The three men pondered the significance of the findings, and while John and Langford speculated, Dr. Christy sat down in a metal armless chair located away from the mortuary table. He sat there for a few moments thinking while Warren pointed out various internal structures to John. While still sitting the doctor began. "There are a few things that are obvious. First, the shot to the chest is the one that killed him or at least it was before he died. With all that blood in the pleural cavity and mediastinum the heart was beating when that bullet went through there. That wound caused him to exsanguinate, or bleed to death, and would have felled him immediately. The bullet wound to the leg must have occurred before the wound to the chest, or at least I don't know why you would shoot somebody in the leg after you had shot them in the chest and killed them."

"There were some tracks of blood, drops of blood out on the road about ten feet before you came upon the body, Doctor," said John. "Apparently he had been running down the road when he was shot and fell."

"That would be it then. He ran down the road and was shot first in the leg; that didn't bring him down and then he was shot again, this time in the chest and through the pulmonary artery. This would bring him down immediately. What this means is that as he lay there someone came up and shot him in the head after he was dead and that explains why there was no blood in the head wound."

"Twice, doctor," interject John. "There were two bullet casings by the body, doctor. Brooks must have stood over him and shot him in the head as he was lying there." The three men stood there in silence glancing at each other, each fully understanding what had happened and its significance.

The doctor continued, "Warren, you better save all the bullets for John; he'll probably need those. I guess you can sign the death certificate as death due to three gun shot wounds, one to head, one to chest and one to leg." The coroner stated that he would complete the death certificate and take it to the courthouse. Langford then called Rumph and had him finish the work to be done on Wardel. The prosecutor and physician left. These two men stood outside; there John related to the doctor the events as he knew them and the details of Ross Brooks' arrest. He also told the doctor about his phone call to Judge Newbold. "They'll be on us like locusts," John continued after telling the doctor the story.

The doctor agreed nodding, "It's a terrible thing but I suppose we'll live through it." Dr. Christy paused, "I wonder why that boy picked out this town?"

Without answering the doctor's question, John continued, "There's nothing we can do but try him, doctor. Brooks bragging about it and all, and there's supposed to be three witnesses, and I'm sure we'll find the gun. There's no question about what happened, not after what we've seen, and we can't very well say Mackel was chained and fell into the river."

"How did the F.B.I. get involved?" asked the doctor.

"I don't know but they were the ones who found him and they were the ones who called Redtop. I'm sure I'll be hearing from them again. I'll find out how they're involved. I've already had some phone calls; it may have been the F.B.I. or maybe some news people, maybe both."

"What did you tell them?"

"Nothing," responded John, "didn't even talk to them. I told Jenny to tell them I wasn't home." The two men parted, resigned to the course of events. John returned home; now it was evening and he inquired of Jenny if there had been anything on the news. She answered, "No," but that there had been two more phone calls. One was a man named Farakshnt—she wasn't sure of the name and it was a peculiar pronunciation. He hadn't said what it was about, long distance though. Jenny was sure the man would call back.

Chapter Three

The next morning, Monday, John was at court for the prelimi-
nary hearing and arraignment of Ross Brooks. The hearing was set
for ten o'clock. At that time Justice of the Peace Charles began with a
motion for John to begin. "Your Honor, the people of Alabama
have here present Ross Brooks charged with first degree murder in
the slaying of Wardel Mackel. As you know, this is a capital offense
and we are sure of his guilt."

The Justice of the Peace turned to Ross Brooks and inquired
whether he had a lawyer. This was the first that John had seen Ross
since the murder. John recognized Ross. He was surprised that Ross
was the murderer. John had thought one of the other, more belliger-
ent locals would have been the arrested. Ross didn't look any differ-
ent from what John had remembered him to be. In fact, if anything,
maybe even a little milder than before. At the question by the Justice
Charles, Ross shook his head negatively.

"Can you afford a lawyer?" asked Justice of the Peace Charles.

Ross shrugged his shoulders as a response, then added, "I'd
have to ask my friends." Ross was instructed by the Justice of the
Peace to get in touch with his friends or his relatives to see if he could
afford to obtain legal counsel. He also informed Ross that if he could
not, the court would appoint an attorney for him. The Justice then
looked at John and Redtop and concluded that they should certainly
be able to finish this business by Wednesday morning, and if an attor-
ney had not been found that he would appoint one then. Redtop
was ordered to return Ross to jail.

41

After the hearing Redtop came across the courthouse to John's office. He had with him a small metal box and Ross' wallet containing a driver's license, the registration to a 1952 black Ford and some folded papers with writings by a thick pencil in the unsure hand of a servitor. Among these papers was a worn photograph of a young girl with a boy, maybe 5 or 6, both smiling, a recorded day of brightness from Ross' past. John looked at the wallet and contents and then asked the Sheriff about the gun.

"I have it!" responded Redtop triumphantly, holding up the box for John to see, "and I have his three friends as well. I can arrest them if you want me to," he said throwing out his chest.

John looked at him in surprise. "You have the gun! How did you get it?"

"We spoke to Brooks and his three friends who were with him. They contradict each other's stories, denying things that they have already said but piecing it together the four of them went to the picnic while it was still going on and made their presence known by the car. It didn't take long before the church members spotted them and started leaving. Somehow or another Wardel ended up out there with the four of them after everyone else had cleared out. The four of them forced Wardel into the car and drove out to right field. There they all got out of the car and they roughed Mackel up a bit, threatened him, with Brooks waving a pistol around and shooting off his mouth. They had all been drinking." Then with a puzzled look, the Sheriff went on, "Then for some reason Mackel broke and started running down the road into the woods. When he did that Brooks shot him, or at least he shot, they think, four times. They heard Mackel stumble and fall and Brooks followed him down the path until he came across him lying there. After two more shots he threw the gun into the woods. I went out there yesterday with the deputies and we found the gun not far from where the body had laid. The gun was empty when I found it." At this Redtop showed John a Rohm RG10 .22 caliber revolver.

Unknown to John and the Sheriff, this weapon had been imported into New York from West Germany in 1956. It was registered to Octavio Mendosa, then of no fixed address in New York City, who was now a resident at Atica State Penitentiary. The gun had travelled south changing owners several times without registration when Ross Brooks had bought it in Chattanooga, Tennessee. It had six chambers and was made of zinc that was slightly pitted.

"I found a box of 22 shots in Brooks' room. Of course, they fit the gun; there must be two other bullets out there somewhere though. I'll send Lester and Jack Hawes out to Mount Zion to find them if they can." Redtop then inquired of John if he had heard anything from the F.B.I. agents. When John responded in the negative, Redtop added, "Good and good riddance to them. Those guys are going to be nothing but trouble to anyone." It was obvious that the two federal men had made Redtop nervous out at Mount Zion field; John added that he didn't think that they had heard the last of them.

"Listen," continued Redtop, "that fellow Mackel was looking for trouble, walking around, strutting, telling everybody what he was going to do, disrupting everything. He had no business here and he got what was expected, and we're a whole lot better off without him."

John did not comment on Redtop's assessment. "Sheriff, keep the gun and see if in fact Brooks owns it and if it's registered anywhere. We have the bullets and by Wednesday Brooks will have a lawyer and we'll take him to the grand jury for indictment. You have the names of the fellows in the car with Brooks?" The Sheriff nodded yes and handed John a paper with the names and I.D. of the three youths with Brooks.

John continued, "Don't charge them with anything, at least for now, but make sure they don't go anywhere."

Redtop made a slight painful grimace, rose, "Yes, sir," and left the room.

The envelope delivered to John's office was not addressed. In the upper left hand corner was a return address, Langford's Funeral Home, Tallawampa, Alabama. Inside the envelope were four metal fragments irregularly shaped and slightly flattened, four twenty-two slugs. John took the envelope with the four bullets and placed them in a larger envelope from his desk. He sealed the larger envelope and wrote on the front, Wardel Mackel. He then placed the envelope in his pocket.

It wasn't eleven in the morning yet, but John had had three phone calls already. One was from Jeremiah Crowley who had left a return number with a Montgomery exchange. John thought that must be the regional office for the F.B.I. The other two calls were from unidentified news men. Both had said they would return their calls. John called the Montgomery exchange. In his conversation with

43

Crowley, the latter offered the services of the F.B.I. in the prosecution of John's case. John formally thanked the agent for his offer and told him that he didn't think it would be necessary. Crowley continued that he understood John's confidence in the matter and that he didn't want to impinge upon John's prerogatives but that there were considerable resources that his office and the agency could make available. Crowley also indicated that if John didn't mind he would like to return to Tallawampa to discuss in further detail some of the forensic expertise that could be made available to him. The two men decided to meet in John's office the next morning at nine-thirty. After the conversation John went to his secretary's desk in the reception room. Dora was a neat, moderately compulsive, thirty-five year old woman who kept Tallawampa's prosecutor's office in order. She was not a glamorous woman but pretty nevertheless. John reminded Dora that he was not taking any phone calls but for her to record all messages. He left his office and went down the stairs to the central foyer of the courthouse. He turned right and used the drinking fountain outside the tax assessor's office. In this trip he saw several persons, two of whom were employees at the courthouse. All three of the persons spoke. There was not a tone in their voices nor a look in their eyes that there was anything different in Tallawampa than there had been for the past five years. As John went back upstairs toward Sheriff Redtop's office, he was confident that these people knew that there had been a murder. When he reached Redtop's office, he entered. Redtop, wearing a smile, asked John again if he wanted to see the prisoner; John shook his head no.

Redtop motioned for Lester to leave the room. John took the envelope from his pocket with the four bullets and informed Redtop that he had received these from Langford, the coroner. Redtop had the twenty-two caliber pistol in his desk drawer ready to be sent for fingerprints to the state laboratory. With the bullets now in custody, the gun could also be sent for ballistics.

"If there is not a chain of custody then these bullets won't be admissible as evidence," stated Redtop looking at the slugs.

"We'll let the court decide what's admissible as evidence. When you have the reports, Sheriff, send them over to my office."

"Yes, sir," Redtop responded without raising his head. John left the Sheriff's office and walked through the courthouse. He paused on the portico, straightened up confidently and began the walk

44

across the courthouse lawn. He met several other persons as he approached Courthouse Square and First Street. He walked down toward Mellons. He entered the restaurant as he had done countless times before, the same tables, the same menu, the same waitress, and the same few faces. There was a slight but demonstrable difference in the affect of the people in the restaurant. He was sure that these people knew about the murder and they also suspected that there was going to be a trial and that he was going to prosecute it. He ate his lunch alone in a friendly environment. The other patrons avoided John but only mildly. After lunch he walked out on First Street; instead of returning to the courthouse he began walking toward Semmes Street. He saw other people in his community as he walked, people he had known all his life. He looked into each face as best he could. They frequently looked the other way after expressing an appropriate greeting. He was sure he saw Dewey Bishop cross to the other side of the street to avoid him, but when the two men were parallel on different sides of First Street, Dewey waved and John followed with a hello. Dewey returned the hello and kept on going. John had planned to go home, get the car and go out to Mount Zion field but he changed his mind; he had already been to Mellon's, maybe he would go to the drugstore and buy a pack of razor blades, anything. He decided to go by dad's store as well—maybe I'll buy a hammer there—and the grocery wouldn't be a bad place to go either.

John started his trek, first to the drugstore, and, as he had planned, he bought the razor blades. The store was nearly empty but the druggist was friendly. After the drugstore, he went back up First Street to what had been his dad's store. It had changed, but not much, and when he walked inside, he noticed the bench in the window well where he used to set the TV. The people at Delta Pride were surprised to see John in the store. "Heavens, what honor do we have, the counselor right here before us." There was a joviality and camaraderie; the few customers in the store looked from behind shelves. They stayed their distance and feined preoccupation with various commodities. The ones he confronted spoke with pleasantness. Each person John saw he thought, 'this might be a juror.' He bought the hammer and there was a great to do about counting out the change of three dollars and twenty-one cents.

He left the store and continued his trip with razor blades and hammer. He continued up Courthouse Square toward the grocery;

there must have been a dozen people in the store including the attendants. Some of them came over to him; each person again said a cordial hello and was friendly. He walked to the produce section and came across Miss Denny, the retired school teacher. He startled the women to embarrassment. She smiled and fluttered away. John picked up a cantaloupe and took it to the checkout counter. The sixteen-year old Prather girl processed his purchase without their eyes meeting. John left and started for home. He walked along armed with blades, hammer and melon; he decided to have the melon for dessert. When he arrived home the door of the house was open as were most of the windows. The house was empty. He went into the kitchen and cut the cataloupe into three pieces. He placed two in the refrigerator and from the third he scooped the seeds into the sink. This portion he set onto a plate and ate in leisure at the kitchen table. He put the spoon, eaten portion of melon and plate in the sink. He picked up the keys to his car, went outside and drove off toward Mount Zion field. He had no real place to go but he just needed time for things to fall into place. He had no particular reason to go to Mount Zion field but that was as good as anyplace to go. As he drove along he thought about the people he had seen in town that day. They all knew about the murder and they all knew now that there had been an autopsy. They also knew there were two F.B.I. agents involved. The people may have been a little nervous, even apprehensive, mildly suspicious but certainly not hostile or frightened. This is the beginning of our troubles, that's what they were thinking and it's going to get worse; I've already won the first round, John decided. Everybody probably knows by now that Dr. Christy had been at the autopsy and everyone knew that the doctor was Judge Newbold's best friend. John reflected about the doctor's participation the day before. It had been Dr. Christy who had done all the talking at the examination of the body. In fact, he was there before John was and had started the autopsy before John had arrived. It had been the doctor who had taken the initiative, and unsolicited; he had told Langford to find the bullet in the leg and to open the track of the bullet's path; and it had been the doctor who had told Langford to collect the bullets and give them to John. He also had put together the sequence of the firings of the shells in their proper order. I'm going to prosecute, John thought to himself. The State of Alabama is going to prosecute and we can win! He speeded up the engine of his car. No sooner. had this burst of enthusiasm come upon him than it left. As he slowed down the engine to a reasonable rate, he asked himself how? This is a capital offense. Alabama has never convicted a white man of killing a negro and God knows they would never electrocute one even if the state law requires it. The answer he continued was to separate the two. Tell the jury never mind the punishment, all we have to do is our part, to find out whether Ross Brooks is guilty or not. We'll let the judge decide what the punishment is and we know the judge will be fair. Instruct the jury that all we have to do is our part. Just do what is right; he came back to making it a contest between himself and Ross Brooks. Isolate him, make the jury pick either John Prichard or Ross Brooks. And if I don't get into any arguments with the defense or the judge and don't give anybody any other alternatives than either one of us, then I should win. John thought about the Sheriff's comment on the nonadmissibility of the bullets as evidence if there was not a proper chain of custody; who needs evidence anyway, everybody in Alabama knows what happened out there, bullets or no bullets, thought John. His mind suddenly shifted to the newspaper men who had called that morning. I know what those devils want, he thought. They are going to lay it all over us, racists, bigots, prosecutor John Prichard! I can see it now. Good God, he continued to think, we even have a Sheriff named Redtop. They'll have his picture on the front page of every paper in the country. I wonder how many messages there will be by this afternoon from those people. Five, he thought, maybe even more. By now he was on Tangent Road approaching Mount Zion field. He pulled off into the picnic area as he had done the morning before. Nothing was there, nothing had changed, just an old abandoned ill-kept colored church, picnic and ball field. He rode as far as the outfield would let him and then stopped the car. It was hot now and the dirt a fine powdered dust. He continued down to the spot where they had found Wardel the day before. There were still traces of blood, black, caked, mixed with the dust. How easily things change. John looked around; he speculated how far he could throw a pistol standing from that spot looking off to the side of the road and into the bushes.

Then it dawned on John—he hadn't seen any of the colored since the murder; he hadn't seen a single one. I wonder what they think. What are they supposed to think, he continued his thoughts.

47

They're back in the woods where they can't be found, hiding in shame or fear and despair. I'll find out what they think; I'll see what they say. John decided he'd drive down by the river. There were always some of those fellows fishing down there; in fact, that's all some of those older fellows could do. He went back to his car and when he reached it he turned looking down Loggen Road once more, put his car in reverse and left Mount Zion field. When he reached Tangent Road he continued southwest toward the river. The road was rough and unimproved. He drove along for another fifteen minutes till he came to an opening by the river bank and sure enough three of those black fellows were fishing there. One of them was Jesse, a cousin of Franklin's. None of the three took any notice of John and made no pretense of recognizing him. The three colored men were not together but were separate, each fishing alone. John walked away from the three down the river as it fell off, under the pretense of examining the current. He knew what they were thinking. This is the way it is: this is the way it's always been and this is the way it's always going to be. When he came back toward his car, John approached the nearest of the elders. "Having any luck? John asked.

"No, sir, no luck today; no, sir, no luck at all." The man sat there not looking at John. He repeated, "Lord, no luck, uhh-uhh, no luck," he continued looking straight ahead.

"Well, that's the way it is some days," said John.

"Lord, yes indeed, yes sir, that's the way it is."

John walked on and approached Jesse. He began with the same introduction as to the last fisherman but Jesse was not obsequious. Jesse kept looking into the river; it was three or four minutes before he began, "He wasn't all that bad, Mr. John, no sir, that boy wasn't all that bad." The two stood there in silence; there was nothing John could do but agree. "No reason for those boys to do what they did, no sir."

He finally added softly, "You're right, Jesse."

"That's awful what they did; there's no call for that at all, none whatsoever." The two men stood there in silence again, John looking at the current. He finally answered again, "You're right, Jesse." After another few moments, John told Jesse he had to be getting back and left.

When John reached his car he headed back toward Tangent Road and town. It was only early afternoon and he wasn't prepared

48

to spend the rest of the afternoon sitting in the office listening to the phone ring. He decided he would drive to Montgomery. It would take him two hours or so each way so he wouldn't be back in the office till late afternoon. He would bypass Tallawampa on his way to Montgomery.

When he returned to his office later that day from Montgomery, John was greeted with, "Where have you been, they've been calling here all afternoon!" He looked at his secretary with some surprise.

"You've had seven calls from newspaper men. One of them called three times, his name was Farakshnt or something like that."

"Did you tell him that I wasn't available?"

"Yes, I told them all that," Dora responded, "but I know they're going to keep on calling. In fact, two of them asked me where Tallawampa was. I told them it was in Alabama," Dora added in mild indignation. "I'm sure they plan to be here," she continued. "Mr. Ketchum from the State's Attorney General's Office called as well." John knew Lynn Ketchum who had been two years ahead of John in law school. When he inquired whether Lynn Ketchum offered any help, Dora answered, "No," then she informed John how Ketchum thought the murder was so regrettable. "He seemed rather concerned about the publicity," Dora continued.

"And he didn't offer any assistance?" Dora responded to the question by shaking her head no.

John picked up his brief case, worn, frayed and with insignificant material inside it. "I'm leaving for the day, Dora. I'll be in in the morning. Record any calls and messages." John decided he would avoid people as well as he could in the few minutes it would take to reach home.

49

Chapter Four

When John arrived home Jenny was standing in the doorway.

"Came home for lunch, I see. What made you do that?"

"Not really lunch, just dessert. I bought a cantaloupe and came home and ate it."

"I'm proud of you"she returned as she kissed him and touched his arm. "You've had some phone calls, one man called twice. It was Mr. Farakshnt again. He said he would be in Tallawampa tomorrow and he wanted to meet with you."

"Well, if anybody calls, tell them I'm not available."

"My, aren't we being mysterious," she said continuing to smile. John returned the smile but didn't answer.

"Do you know what you're doing?" she continued inquisitively.

"I hope so," John nodded with a smile.

They ate a cold dinner of shrimp, rice, green peppers, tomatoes and iced tea. John spent the evening milling about the house. There were four calls that evening and Jenny answered them all. Two of them were for her; with one of the other calls Jenny was evasive and at several points of the conversation even stammered. She would attempt to answer a question and before she could complete her statement there had obviously been another question. Finally, she said, "Why no, we don't have a hotel here in Tallawampa. I will certainly tell my husband you called." It must be Farakshnt, thought John as he continued with his civil war papers.

Both John and Jenny watched the six and ten o'clock news that evening. Both newscasts came from the local station WABA in

50

Montgomery. On the local news there was an announcement of Wardel Mackel's murder. "A twenty-year old youth from Detroit was killed during an altercation on Sunday at a baseball game in Tallawampa. There are reasons to believe the murder was racially motivated. A suspect has been arrested." There was no other information available about Tallawampa or the murder. The news from the national networks had been much as they had been before. There was no mention about Tallawampa's murder.

John awakened early the next morning and Farakshnt was on his mind. Curious name he thought. Both Dora and Jenny remembered him and of all the callers he was easily the most persistent. He had to be a newspaper man, John thought. John half dressed and fixed coffee; he took the second slice of melon from the icebox. He then walked down to the gate to pick up his morning newspaper. He unfolded the paper as soon as he took it out of the box and there were the headlines—"Local Youth Arrested In Sunday Murder." Beneath the headlines there was the item, "William Marmande to Defend Suspect." John didn't pause; he didn't stop and he didn't read any further. He stood there in the middle of his walkway, lowered the paper and looked around the yard. "William Marmande," he said aloud. "How did that boy do that? How did that boy get William Marmande to defend him, good God!" he repeated out loud. He repeated the name, William Marmande, to himself. John continued, any number of fellows that hang around the courthouse would have suited this bill, but William Marmande, he was the best lawyer in these parts and the only people who knew it were the judges and lawyers. John returned into the house and read the article about the murder and Ross Brooks. There was nothing in the story about Ross bragging of the shooting, and there was nothing mentioned about the three witnesses. The autopsy was mentioned but the sequence of the shots were not described. In the article there were considerable pains taken to describe Ross as the accused and no more. When John finished reading the article, his thoughts returned to William Marmande. Just incredible, he thought. I wonder who told Brooks about William Marmande. Certainly not Judge Newbold nor the lawyers, they wouldn't. The lawyers would have kept the case for themselves. And William Marmande was not the type to go around looking for cases. In fact, he stayed so far back in the woods you could hardly find him and now he's coming to Tallawampa to defend

51

this kid. This was more than John could believe.

William Marmande lived over in Washington County. He was reputed to have great wealth but John doubted this—William Marmande loved the law, not money. He was a trial lawyer—obfuscation and guile, creating doubt and fears about torts and administrative regulations in third parties was not in William Marmande. His work was involved in proving innocence or guilt, not furtivity; therefore, he spent most of his time in the courtroom.

There were only two times that William had been in Tallawampa to try cases that John could remember. One was while John was still in his third year of law school. That summer he went to the courthouse when court was in session to observe the proceedings. William Marmande had been hired to defend Jack Whitney who had embezzled twenty-two thousand dollars from the local Tallawampa bank. There was great publicity and stir about the case. Twenty-two thousand dollars might not be much money to some people but it was a ton of money in Tallawampa. Josh Davis was the prosecuting attorney at that time and when Whitney came to court charged with embezzlement and feloneous grand theft, it was an obvious case with an obvious conclusion. They had found four thousand dollars of the embezzled money in Jack Whitney's home and another two thousand dollars of the money in Jack Whitney's savings account in the same Tallawampa bank. But when the prosecutor rested his case William Marmande stood in his rumpled suit and approached the bench with compassion in his eyes and a tremble in his voice. He began, "Your Honor, I fear there's been a grave misunderstanding here, and the charges against my client have been misrepresented. My client is not a felon and he has not stolen twenty-two thousand dollars as is alleged."

Everyone in the courtroom gazed in disbelief and Judge Newbold asked, "Mr. Marmande, are you denying the charges," and when William had responded that he was, the Judge continued, "Mr. Marmande, the prosecutor has put into evidence records indicating that Mr. Whitney stole twenty-two thousand dollars and you made no objection to this." The Judge continued, "These records are ledgers from the bank, not forged, and they are on the bank's stationary. They are signed by Mr. Whitney himself and also by the bank officials and the bank examiners. I don't know how—" When the Judge paused, William Marmande began.

"Your Honor, if I may, these records indicate that my client stole twenty dollars, eleven hundred times. Not that he stole twenty-two thousand dollars. There's a big difference as he is charged; the theft of twenty-two thousand dollars is a serious crime and a felony, but what my client actually did was a succession of misdemeanors. What he is guilty of is theft of an insignificant amount of money many times. Your Honor, this is a series of misdemeanors and my client should stand charged for them, not for a felony."

Then prosecutor Josh Davis blew his stack. "Your Honor, this is trickery. This man stole twenty-two thousand dollars," he hollered.

"Your Honor, taking a sleeping pill every night of the year is one thing but taking three hundred sixty-five sleeping pills on one night is quite a different thing and has quite a different consequence."

Before William Marmande could continue, Josh Davis roared out again, "He stole twenty-two thousand dollars." But William Marmande and Judge Newbold would have no part of it. The prosecutor had laboriously put into evidence page after page of the bank records indicating that Jack Whitney had shorted the bank twenty dollars a day for nearly four and a half years.

"Your point is well taken, Mr. Marmande," stated the Judge. Judge Newbold glanced at the prosecuting attorney and looked away quickly. Then William Marmande approached the bench and informed the Judge that Mr. Whitney had family in Texas. There was a huddle before the Judge's bench of the two lawyers and the Judge. "You say he has family in Texas?"

"Yes, he does, your Honor." That evening Jack Whitney was on the train and not to be seen again in Tallawampa.

The second case that William Marmande had tried in Tallawampa was that of Billy Bumphries who, at nineteen on moonlit autumn nights, had burned down eleven farmers' barns. Those were barns filled with produce, livestock and equipment that represented not only a whole year' backbreaking work for those farmers but also much of their resources. If those farmers and their families were to have anything that year, it was going to come out of those barns. There was no surer road to a lengthy term in the state penitentiary than to set fire to a barn in that rural agricultural community. When Billy Bumphries came into court that day before a jury of agrarians, his fate was as sealed as that of a yule log at Christmas time. Those farmers would have no compassion or inclination for clemency for

Billy Bumphries. The prosecutor at that time was now state senator, Doyle Nicks. Doyle presented his case very deliberately. He had the dates, the places, and he had the witnesses; he had records of Billy buying the gasoline. He had the testimony of the attendant who sold the gasoline. He even produced the four cans that Billy had bought (in Prichard's store) that he used to carry the gas to the various barns. Two of the cans were found at different barns, two at Billy's home, and then there were eye witnesses to two of the burnings. To nail down an already airtight case, Doyle next came forth with a signed confession from Billy Bumphries. The state rested its case and as it did, Doyle took his seat with a flair and confidence of having served his citizens well. After he was comfortably seated, William Marmande rose and approached the bench. It was the same compassionate expression and deep low modulated voice—a voice that called for reason.

"Your Honor," he began, "it would be difficult for me to refute such comprehensively presented evidence that the prosecutor has put forward for us today. However, I would like to present the results of five tests that have been performed on the defendant by experts from the University of Alabama. I can produce these experts, if desired, or I can present the results of these tests, if it's agreeable to the Court." With no objections, William continued. He withdrew multiple papers from his briefcase and began. "The first of these is the SRA student reference assessment test which was performed on Billy Bumphries on November the 16th. This test evaluates the academic achievement of people and classifies them in grade level as to year and month. The test also compares each individual with peers of his own age and ranks them in a percentile compared to his peers. This test was administered under the auspices of the University of Alabama's Education Department, and, as you can see from the score, places Billy Bumphries at the fourth grade, fifth month level."

The prosecutor, Doyle Nicks, interrupted, "Your Honor, I don't see where this has anything to do with setting fires. Nobody has said that you have to be smart to light a match." Laughter filled the room. Judge Newbold raised his hand and silence prevailed, he then motioned for William Marmande to continue. "The same test puts my client at the third percentile compared with peers of his own age. Your Honor, the second test I have is the Appledeen standard psychological emotional test; this test is prepared by the University of

54

California and is used throughout the country. It is used to evaluate the psychological, social and emotional development of individuals and places them both at an age level as well as a percentile when compared with their peers of the same age. This test was given to Billy Bumphries again on November 16th of this year under the auspices of the University of Alabama and shows that Billy Bumphries is psychologically nine years old, and, as compared to his peers, that is, other nineteen-year olds, he is in the second percentile."

The prosecutor Doyle Nicks interrupted again, this time exasperated. "Your Honor if the defense is saying Billy Bumphries is nuts, let him so state it and put on a psychiatrist to prove it."

William Marmande continued, "Your Honor, I'm not saying that Billy Bumphries is nuts, and I would like to continue presenting my evidence."

Thomas Newbold nodded for William Marmande to continue.

"Your Honor, the third test I have is the emotional adaptation test which was developed by the University of Tennessee, and this measures only the emotional development of the person and again it measures a person's age level and compares them as a percentile to people of the same chronological age. This test was given to Billy Bumphries also on November 16th and again under the auspices of the University of Alabama. He scored on this test eight years, tenth month, and, compared with his peers of the same chronological age, he was determined to be in the fourth percentile. The last test, your Honor, is the standard I.Q. test that measure the intellectual quotient of individuals and this test was given the next day on November the 17th and again under the auspices of the University of Alabama. My client scored on this test, 77. This number of correct answers is the same as students in the fourth grade, second month. Your Honor, the defense concedes that Billy Bumphries is nineteen years old chronologically and that the statutes of the criminal code for the state are determined on a chronological age; however, by any and all measures of testing the defendant is academically, psychologically, socially, emotionally and intellectually to be no way near that of an adult or nineteen-year old. He is, at best, a young child. In fact, he is barely a nine-year old. I do not maintain that he is crazy but that he is severely wanting and when examined in light of the needs necessary for life and by all the standards and measures we have available, we are dealing with an elementary school child. The jail is no place for such a person so young. I would like to move for a judgment of acquittal on the grounds of impaired mental capacity and the defendant be sent for counseling to a special school so that proper diagnostic and therapeutic procedures can be performed to assist in his maturation and development."

There was not sound in the courtroom. Thomas Newbold looked at the prosecutor and the prosecutor looked back at Thomas. They both looked at Billy Bumphries who was oblivious to the proceedings of which he was a part. The Judge's eyes touched on the ceiling and he scanned various objects in the room quickly. He glanced at the jury who were as dumbfounded as the prosecutor. The Judge then returned to William Marmande, "Counselor, you have made a good point. Have you made any arrangements for such counseling and educational services to help the defendant."

"Yes, I have, your Honor," added William quickly. "There is a wonderful school in Abilene, Texas." The next morning Billy Bumphries was on his way to Texas to some school of some description to help him mature. Doyle Nicks is still probably trying to figure out what happened that day, John thought as he continued his coffee.

William Marmande must be 53, maybe 54, thought John, maybe even older. He was from down on the Gulf Coast and he had gone to school in New Orleans. He had offices in both Mobile and Washington County; he lived in the latter with his wife; they had one child, a son who was a dentist who practiced in Bay St. Louis. Everyone in these parts knew William Marmande or at least knew who he was; but John wasn't sure who his friends were. Everybody was his friend. He certainly didn't hang around the courthouse. He wasn't that type. He belonged to the Bar Association but did not participate in its activities. William Marmande added a new dimension to the case. This isn't going to be a trial; this is going to be a match and murder to boot! A capital offense, thought John. Both of those case that William Marmande had tried in Tallawampa, the defendants were guilty and the prosecutors had all the evidence; and both the defendants were free and never went to jail. What William Marmande had done for Jack Whitney and Billy Bumphries he would also try to do for Ross Brooks. William knew the law and also how to use it to his client's advantage. John knew the mistake that both of those prosecutors had made against William in those earlier cases. They had spent too much time proving their cases and proving something that everybody already knew. Neither of those prosecutors isolated the defendant, separating them from everybody else. They hadn't made it a contest where there would be a winner and a loser; nor had they placed the defendant in the circumstances where he couldn't win. William Marmande added a new dimension to the case all right; nobody beat William Marmande in the courtroom and now John was going to have a chance to go against him, the number one lawyer, and in a murder one case at that! He hurried upstairs to awaken Jenny.

"Honey, I have to go to Mobile on business." It wasn't even eight o'clock.

The aroused and sleepy Jenny asked, "Mobile on business?"

He didn't give her a chance to continue, "Just on business; I don't have time to eat. I want to leave now; I'll be back sometime this afternoon, and don't tell anyone where I'm going." John hurriedly finished dressing and left the house. He went out Semmes Street past the cemetery where the road connected to Route 24 and headed for Mobile. It would be almost two hours to Mobile; it's a shame that I had shrimp last night, maybe I'll have speckled trout for lunch. Anyway, it was going to be a great day. I'll go down to Wentzel's. Maybe I can make it as far as the Fairgrounds and go to the track. He dismissed the case from his mind. Enough of that for now, he thought. This will be a day of rest.

John returned late in the afternoon from Mobile and went straight to his office. Dora began the same way, "Where have you been, Mr. Prichard. You missed your appointment with Mr. Crowley, the F.B.I. agent, and he waited here for two hours. I finally called your wife, and she said that you had been called out of town unexpectedly. When she said that she didn't know when you would be back, I didn't know what to do. He waited here until noon time; he didn't say anything but I could tell he was upset. He left his number again and said that he would call you; and this phone has been ringing all day and any number of people have called you about this case. I'm sure they mean business. I had everything to do to apologize to them when I couldn't tell them where you were or when you would be in. I have a whole list of names here for you to call with numbers; some of them are staying in Montgomery and a few of them as far away as Birmingham. I know they aren't going to take 'no' for an answer. They want some explanations and they mean business." John looked at the list of names that his secretary handed him. There was Crowley's name at the top; he walked into his office and dialed the F.B.I. office in Montgomery. Crowley was subdued and paused on the phone waiting for John to begin with his apologies. "I was called away unexpectedly. I'm terribly sorry about our appointment this morning, and I certainly didn't mean to inconvenience you in any way. I ask a thousand pardons for you having to travel all the way here to Tallawampa and then me not being here." John assured the federal agent that he hadn't been idle in the case. "We've had our preliminary hearing and the defendant has an attorney. We'll meet tomorrow for the arraignment, and I may be able to present it to the grand jury this week or the first part of next week. Tomorrow morning I'll be in court for the arraignment. Would you like to meet tomorrow afternoon."

Crowley accepted John's apologies for his absence, and the two men again decided that tomorrow afternoon, Wednesday afternoon, would be an appropriate time to meet. They both agreed on 1:30.

John looked over the list of names Dora had given him. Farakshnt was there with three checks beside it. Dora walked into his office to bring John some more information. When she entered he asked her, "What do you think about all this, Dora?"

"The murder you mean?" she looked at him startled, surprised that he had asked her opinion.

"Yes," responded John.

"A murder is a sin against God, it's right in the Bible." Dora began, "The fifth commandment says, 'Thou shalt not kill'. In Exodus, 21st chapter, 12th verse, 'he that strikest a man with a will to kill him, shall be put to death." There followed a profuse litany of prophets and evangelists, each establishing beyond doubt the evil and guilt of murder. "Wait," Dora said, she quickly went to her desk and brought back a bible concordance frequently used and heavily underlined. She flipped through the pages of cross indexes damning murder. "Look here," she said, "in Deuteronomy, chapter 19." Before she could read further John interjected meekley, "I suppose you're right, Dora; I suppose I'll have to answer all those phone calls too." How could he get Dora on the jury he thought, asking himself in jest; no way "Dora, we'll continue tomorrow."

When John reached home, Jenny was standing in the doorway

58

again waiting for him as he came up the walkway. "Are they still talking to you at the courthouse?" she began.

"Some of them are," he answered.

"I'm serious," she continued emphatically but with a lightness in her voice. "I have turf to defend; I have to know what's going on; I can't participate in this lightly," she again said smiling but with emphasis. John walked past her and she followed him into the kitchen. She pressed her cause. "I have to know these things, I have responsibilities," she again said continuing to smile. They stood in the kitchen without speaking, looking, admiring each another.

Finally, he began, "Well they speak, you know, they talk, just hints, no more, whispers mostly."

"Hints of what," she said with alarm She then lowered her eyes, "You love what you're doing."

"Um, something like that."

"Good!" she responded. Jenny prepared dinner, and John poured iced tea.

During dinner there was a phone call from Farakshnt. Jenny answered the phone and told Mr. Farakshnt that John was not in but would be back at nine o'clock. If he called then she was sure that John would be there. The two of them finished their dinner and sat in their living room watching the evening news. It was a pleasant room with six windows. This allowed in light in the morning, afternoon and evening. There was a couch and two chairs facing the nineteen-inch television screen. Beyond the screen there was a single window that faced east. On the same wall was a fireplace used infrequently but one of the delights of the Prichard's home. There were two geese decoys on the mantle. On the opposite wall were bookshelves with volumns ranging from antiques to Zeus, arranged with no pretense of alphabetical order. In a few moments flashing began and a voice with great poise and diction started, "Civil rights activities continued throughout the South and among these activities included the murder of one civil rights activist in Tallawampa, Alabama, gunned down by a racist assailant while at prayer at a church picnic. Elsewhere throughout the South, there was ever escalating violence against those seeking civil rights." The news continued but was anticlimatic as far as Tallawampa, John and Jenny were concerned. They didn't discuss the news as they both stumbled about the house. John went back to his papers on the Civil War battle of

Gravelly Springs. He also looked into his papers on packet ships that served on the Black Hawk River. At nine sharp the phone rang. Jenny answered the phone and quickly handed it to John. He held the phone to his ear without speaking and listened a moment, then two. There was not a sound. Finally, after several moments, John began, "Yes."

"Is this John Prichard?" a voice demanded. When assured that it was, the voice continued, "This is Jack Farakshnt, and I'm with the New York Times. I've called you twenty-seven times in the last three days, and you haven't returned one of my calls or even acknowledge any of my inquiries. But never mind that, my interest in calling you is the recent murder that occurred in your jurisdiction, and I understand that you are the prosecuting attorney. I would like to discuss the case with you." John interrupted at this point.

"Well, I'm not in the practice of discussing business on the phone."

"This isn't business I'm discussing, it's murder. I expect to be in Tallawampa tomorrow morning, but I'm told there is no place to stay, that there are no motels or hotels there. I would like to stay in your house."

"My house?" John said.

"Yes, at your house, god-damm it." Even John was surprised; he hadn't anticipated this. "Well, I'm sorry but we don't rent rooms. We did at one time but we don't rent them anymore so there is no way we can possibly do that." Farakshnt passed off the rebuff as anticipated.

"Never mind, I'll stay in Montgomery, and I'll visit you in the morning at your office at nine-thirty."

John responded, "I'll be in court tomorrow morning at nine-thirty, Mr. Farakshnt. Perhaps you might call my secretary and state the nature of your business and we'll arrange for a mutually convenient time to meet."

"You know the nature of my business, I just told you I'm a newspaper man, and I'm investigating the murder of Wardel Mackel of which you are responsible for the prosecution."

John interrupted, "Mr. Farakshnt, I'm not in the habit of discussing my cases before I prosecute them, and if you're interested in records, all of our records and documents are kept in the courthouse, and you're welcome to review any of the records that we have concerning any case." In the middle of John's statement, Farakshnt exploded, "Courthouse records in Alabama! What the hell is the matter with you; do you think I'm nuts?" There was another pause.

"I'm not sure what you're referring to, Mr. Farakshnt, but there's no more valid records of public evidence that you can find than in a county courthouse." There was a total silence after John's comments. Farakshnt was obviously at a loss for words. John knew what he was thinking—I'll beat your bloody brains out. The pause continued. Farakshnt didn't respond. John finally continued, "Perhaps you could call my office and arrange for an appointment, Mr. Farakshnt. Do you have my number? Mr. Farakshnt, it's Alabama 1212. Did you get that, Mr. Farakshnt, Alabama 1212." There was still silence. Finally, there was a slow deliberate response, "I have your number, Mr. Prichard. I'll call you in the morning; I'll call you in the morning." He hung up the phone without a complimentary closing.

John went back to his civil war papers. He pulled out correspondence he had with a family in Oblong, Illinois concerning the battle of Gravelly Springs. His mind quickly left Gravelly Springs though; he was already looking forward to the arraignment and the meeting with Jeremiah Crowley he had scheduled for the next day. He was sure Farakshnt would be in Tallawampa tomorrow as well.

But tomorrow there would be another meeting in Tallawampa, a meeting of equal importance to the arraignment and those in the prosecutor's office, and that was Tallawampa's monthly meeting of the United Daughters of the Confederacy. This group of graying women were determined to perpetuate their devotions and loyalties to a gradually diminishing number of younger conferees. This group, together with the Garden club, were the two citadels of Tallawampa's ladies. Comfort Newbold, the judge's wife, was the president of the Garden Club, and Amy Swain was the current president of the Daughters. There was nothing that was going to happen in Tallawampa without the approval of these two groups. The meeting for tomorrow would be at Amy Swain's house which meant that all of Tallawampa's proper ladies would be there. John casually asked Jenny whether she planned to attend. She was somewhat surprised by John's inquiry and informed him that she would not dare miss a meeting at Amy Swain's.

The continuance for counsel for Ross Brooks was set for 9:30.

At the designated time all persons were in their places and ready for their participation. The magistrate was again Justice of the Peace Charles. John had never met William Marmande before but he went over to the defendant's bench and William introduced himself and called John by name. William had a pleasant engraciating smile and a face that people instinctively liked. The two men exchanged a few pleasantries. In a moment the Clerk of the Court called for order as the magistrate entered the room and the bailiff produced Ross Brooks. The room was crowded, not packed, but there must have been 40 local people there, as well as a number of outsiders. The magistrate viewed the room and the gallery with interest. He began, "We met day before yesterday for the presentation of one Ross Brooks, here in attendance for a consideration to be presented to the grand jury. At that time he did not have counsel and was so instructed to obtain counsel or the court would appoint same. Do you now," the magistrate looked at Ross, "have—"

William Marmande arose and spoke, "Your Honor, I am William Marmande and I represent the defendant, Ross Brooks."

As William stood the magistrate continued, "Mr. Marmande, your client has been arrested and the prosecutor indicates that he would like to present this case to the grand jury for first degree murder. Because of the seriousness of this crime, I would like first to consider bond in this case." With these words he looked at John.

John rose, "Your Honor, because of the seriousness of this crime of first degree murder, and because the defendant has a past record of imprisonment, I would like to request no bond be set and that he be retained in the custody of the sheriff."

Before the magistrate could begin, William Marmande continued, "Your Honor, if the prosecutor wishes to establish no bond in this case I have no objection, if he thinks it's necessary to the cause of justice."

The magistrate looked at both John and William satisfied that the issue of bond had been resolved, and resolved easily. He continued, "If that's the case, there is no bond and the bailiff can return the defendant to the jail. The grand jury is in session now and when would you want this presented to the grand jury?", he asked looking at John.

John began, "Your Honor, again because of the seriousness of the offense and not to serve the defendant any undue hardship, I

62

would like to have this presented to the grand jury as soon as possible."

"I've no objection with that," William Marmande added.

The magistrate continued again, pleased by the lack of contention, "Then we will have the presentation to the grand jury as soon as possible. I don't know what their schedule is." He then instructed one of the deputies (Jack Hawes) to go ask the Clerk of the Court what was the earliest it could be presented to the grand jury. In a few moments Jack returned. "Friday," Jack announced from the back of the courtroom.

"That is two days hence; it will be presented to the grand jury on Friday." He surveyed both lawyers and they both indicated agreement. "So be it. Friday will be the presentation to the grand jury in the case of Ross Brooks, first degree murder of Wardel Mackel, State of Alabama prosecuting." The Justice of the Peace rapped on his bench and everyone rose. There was a flurry of papers and a murmur of voices.

In the back of the room throughout the hearing there had been a large Semitic man with an intense glare at the proceedings and the people in the room. As John left the courtroom several other men approached him introducing themselves. They were people from out of town covering the murder and they asked John an assortment of questions concerning the evidence in the prosecution of the case. He declined to comment on any of the questions saying it would be improper for him to speculate. "My presentation will be in the courtroom," he added. The Semitic man stayed on the periphery of this group. John wanted to talk to William Marmande but in his distractions by Tallawampa's visitors, William had left.

That afternoon was spent with two meetings—one, Crowley from the F.B.I. and the other, Farakshnt, who it turned out was the Semitic man in the courtroom. Crowley again presented a willingness of the F.B.I. to offer its services. He went through an elaboration of the technical, criminalogical, and forensic services that they could provide. Fingerprinting, ballistics, expert witnesses, legal counsel, and the incorporation of other justice department officials in the prosecution of civil rights cases. John was civil, polite and less than formal with Crowley. Crowley had an openness, a freshness and an honesty that John admired and decided would be of good use. Crowley expressed disappointment, through his facial expressions,

63

as well as words in John not accepting his offers of assistance. But the meeting was cordial and both men left with confidence between them.

The meeting with Farakshnt was something else. John kept him waiting in his reception room for 30 minutes. When he finally came into John's office, he began by asking John what organizations he belonged to. When John responded, "Do you mean churches?" the tone for their relationship was established. Farakshnt continued with similar questions but each question brought an evasive response. John soon answered every question with a vague legalism and before long could hear himself repeating again and again, "Only the court can decide that." The meeting had started with static and soon progressed to sparks. John was uncomfortable, squarmed in his chair, then began excusing himself for no reason to go out to Dora's desk. After several of these feined interruptions, he finally returned and told Farakshnt that he had to be excused, something had happened that needed his immediate attention. "We will have to continue tomorrow, Mr. Farakshnt; a thousand pardons; I should be in first thing in the morning." John left Farakshnt sitting in his office and hurriedly exited. Why am I so nervous and running from my own office, John thought as he went down the stairs two at a time.

By the time John reached home he was relaxed. Jenny was in the kitchen. She began, "Well, I am happy to tell you that the Confederacy lives on in her daughters!"

"Did you have a nice meeting?"

"Yes, delightful. And of course at Amy Swain's everyone was there. I think that's the largest crowd we've had in two or three years."

"Did anything about the trial come up?"

"Not a word. There was more talk about the Garden Club than anything and there was a report on the azalea festival; we've already started on the antiques sale for this fall, and I am pleased to tell you we have over $1,000 in our scholarship fund; and none other than Amy Swain herself informed the members although her mother told her, 'Though we are broke, we are proud!' Today we are still proud, but are no longer broke."

"Of course Comfort Newbold was there; I had a nice talk with her. Besides a pie top table she is going to donate an iron kettle and wooden frame used for making soap for the antique fair. Did you know that the judge's mother made her own soap, and that they didn't buy any food at all. I mean, that woman, the judge's mother, canned, preserved, stored or cooked every bean, tomato and vegetable that they didn't sell. She even cured her own meats and made her own sausages," and with emphases, "besides that, she made her own brooms." Jenny was clearly overwhelmed and shuddered, "Thank God for the 60's!"

They filled in each other on their days. John told Jenny about his meetings with Farakshnt and Crowley as well as William Marmande. "I like them," he added. After dinner they continued their discussions and John returned to Jenny's meeting.

"Was everyone polite at the meeting?" he asked.

"Of course," responded Jenny with a pretense of definance. "And good they should be. And woe to those who would tamper with a descendant of Thomas Holcombe."

With the mention of the ancestor, John turned his head with a look of here we go. "Oh, my lord," he moaned.

"Yes," said Jenny seeing her opportunity; she was going to have her round. "His presence is in this room; you can feel it, his strength, his determination, Frayser's Farm is hallowed, Thomas Holcombe lives!" She was on a roll, she loved it. John held his head, thumped his hands on the arm of the couch, Jenny continued. John fell back on the couch and pulled up his feet assuming a fetal position; he moaned again.

"Yes, the Holcombe's rule," she said as she pried his arms away from his body in a prelude to forepleasure.

On Friday morning, two days later, the grand jury met as scheduled. At the deliberations Redtop, at John's direction, recounted the incidents of Wardel Mackel's shooting and the subequent arrest of Ross Brooks. His presentation was less than thirty minutes and an indictment was returned to try Ross for the murder of Wardel. On the following Monday Ross was in court with his counsel, William Marmande, for the indictment. Ross looked insignificant standing next to the larger Marmande. He also had his hair cut since his last appearance in the courtroom. When the indictment was read, William responded to the charges, "not guilty." Ross was returned to his cell and a trial date was set three weeks hence with Judge Thomas Newbold presiding.

65

Chapter Five

John didn't need three weeks to prepare his case; he already knew what he was going to say and what evidence he was going to present. But this would take some cooperation from a number of third parties. He would have to establish their proper participation and appropriate responses. Some of them would be easier than others. These three weeks were valuable and they also proved to be interesting.

During this pretrial interlude there were numerous new people in town. John didn't get to meet them all but he did meet most of them. One crowd that was conspicuously absent though, were the state attorney general's office, as well as the state politicians. If they made their presence known in Tallawampa, it wasn't to John; those people ran from Tallawampa as far and as fast as they could. Perhaps the governor spoke with Judge Newbold but no one would ever know that. Lynn Ketchum from the state attorney's office never called again. Sheriff Redtop was not himself and avoided John—not hostile but unsure of their relationship. John thought someone from the state may be talking to Redtop; but none of those persons were talking to John. Those state people were probably waiting for him to make the first move. But there wasn't any move for John to make. The criminal statutes were known, the courthouse is here, I have the evidence, and everybody knows what happened. If John sought advice and recommendations from them, the trial would last two years and they would argue over every comma in the criminal code before it would be over. John was confident without the state's help. Perhaps the state was equally confident.

There were two other groups in town and these two groups had similarities as well as differences. They were similar in that they were both determined to get Ross Brooks convicted, and different in that one of them had their hands tied and were powerless, while the other had total lead way and freedom to do as they saw fit. The first group were people from the Justice Department in Washington. The murder had violated a state law, not a federal one, much to the distress of some people. Federal authority was not applicable here since no federal laws had been broken; there was nothing they could do and no way they could intrude. If they wanted to, they could investigate the trial and how it was handled; but there had been nothing broken for them to initiate charges. They could record the events and methods of the proceedings in the murder trial to see what might be necessary to include in some type of future considered federal legislation, but no more than that.

The federal me had as their intermediary Jeremiah Crowley of the regional F.B.I. office. John had developed good rapport with Crowley who had continued to offer John expertise of multiple forensic natures, offers that John continued to decline. But trust continued between these two men. John's refusals were not based on the fact that Crowley's services were not wanted but that they were not needed. Before long Crowley was as convinced of this as John was.

There was also a new sense of trust from the town's people to John during that time. Everyone was sure that things would turn out for the best. "After all, we elected John to do this job. We wouldn't have chosen him if we didn't think he would do what was right. He was correct in having the trial as soon as possible. We'll wrap this up and go onto other things." A tighter bond of friendship prevailed that everything would turn out for the best.

On the two weekends before the trial, John and Jenny left town. One weekend they went to Pensacola, the other to Biloxi. They went as tourists to both cities.

During the weekdays John spent his time in preparation for his presentation. He wrote out the sequence of the witnesses he would call, the questions he would ask each; he decided where to stand when he asked each witness their questions. He thought the proper order of the witnesses was critical to his case. Every detail of the trial and possible alternatives he planned for.

The rest of his time John spent with the second group that was new to Tallawampa, the news media. These were men who, like himself, lived by their wits, insights, probes and the detection of feelings from facial expressions. These men could ferret a prey as quickly as anyone and John was fair game for them.

They were gentlemen—white shirts, ties, jackets and clean hands. But they were tough men with keen insights and persistences. They were mannered when they had to be or when they wanted to be. They lead a circling engagement on Tallawampa. They attacked from all sides and the courthouse was the fort they were out to capture; it seemed to John that they thought the prosecutor's office was the command post. They hammered away from various angles but John limited his discussions to only two things: first, the criminal statutes of Alabama, and second, that he would not discuss any of the evidence of the case. There was no way some newspaper man from up north was going to outsmart him on the criminal laws of Alabama. Since he had all the evidence and wouldn't discuss it, there was no way that they could pry in; and, if Redtop dared to talk to one of them, John vowed he would bury him in quicksand.

They tried repeatedly to get John onto other topics—his views on capital punishment, his ideas on social justice, voting rights, integration of the schools, the role of the federal government in taxation, the quality of education in Alabama, his political loyalties in the state and nation, what did he feel about incidents that had occurred recently in other states. But there was no pinning him down. His was total and absolute evasion with no hints on how he felt about any of these issues. They probed into Mackel's background as well as Ross Brooks' and by this they provided John with information about both those people that he didn't have before.

John allowed only one press conference during the three weeks. The newsmen had wanted it held in front of the courthouse but John had insisted that it be held in his office and with no cameras. Thirty to thirty-five of them squeezed into the prosecutor's office. John was pleased with the way he handled them. The questions were so fast and came from so many persons at once that he could easily select the questions he wanted to answer. He would then talk on nothingness for as long as he liked. It was soon apparent that they were getting nowhere. At the press conference he mixed what he hoped was a proper balance of timidity, evasion, suspicion, and contempt with just a rare spark of determination to insure their continued probing.

John had indicated that home was off limits—no discussions and no calls; but in the office they continued their assault. They asked about both Judge Newbold and William Marmande. "The Judge and I both work at the courthouse. Yes, I've known him all my life," and no more than that. "William Marmande is a fine lawyer," and that was all. If those men approached either the Judge or William Marmande they didn't indicate it to John. The Judge, it turned out, they had not approached out of an appropriate respect and sensitivity. William Marmande they must have just written off. "What would we get from some backwoods lawyer defending the likes of Ross Brooks." Also, William was from Washington County; that was 30 miles from the courthouse. If anybody cared, the only time that William was in Tallawampa those days before the trial was between 6:00 and 6:30 each morning during his daily visit with his client in the county jail.

John had agreed to individual interviews with several of the newsmen. Out of these 7 or 8 he had picked Jack Farakshnt as his main conduit. Jack hammered away not only with greater persistence than the other reporters but also with more directness. There were fewer attempts at entrapment with Farakshnt. with him it was a frontal assault. Farakshnt was prejudiced against the south, but he believed what he felt. John never challenged Farakshnt on this prejudice issue. Farakshnt was also more analytical than the others. There was more direction to his inquiries and greater progression to his thought processes. John was amazed with the scope of his knowledge. On numerous occasions John would interrupt the interview with, "How did you know that?"

"Know what? That, that Mackel was shot?" Jack would answer.

"No, no, not that. You said a few minutes ago that the mayor of Seattle's name was Kover."

"I was there last year," and then again immediately back to Tallawampa.

One morning Jack compared Ross Brooks to Tamerlane. John was flabbergasted. "How did you know about Tamerlane?"

"Everybody knows about Tamerlane," Jack answered. "You know they found his sarcophagus."

69

"They did! Who did?" asked John excited and in disbelief. "Sure, the Russians."

"The Russians!"

"Sure the Russians found it during the Second World War in 1941. It's located in Samarkand. And what do you suppose they found when they opened the lid?"

"I don't know," John answered in anticipation.

"A skeleton of a man with one leg shorter than the other—'Timur the lame'. But he was like Genghis Khan and all those tartars, blood thirsty." John tried to contain his amazement. Then it was quickly back to Tallawampa and the murder; but still more evasions and more circumvention from John. There was an ambivalent pattern established by John. There was never the admission that Jack wanted; there was never the final step that established that John was a racist. Whenever they approached that precipice John would duck behind the courts—"Only the courts can decide cases like this Mr. Farakshnt." John would draw the words out slowly. "The courts, only the courts, can decide that." It infuriated Farakshnt. Jack was up against a stone wall with "the courts". It was the court that would decide, and there was no alternative. If you didn't like what they ruled, there was nothing to do, maybe appeal; but it would still be "the courts decide". How can you change a court that you don't have any jurisdiction over—the judge, the prosecutor, the jury, the codes; there was no way to change these things and Jack felt caught and bound But this was only the first inning. If events in this case were beyond Jack's control, it was then his function to make sure that it wouldn't happen again. Jack wasn't without means to disseminate information and influence. His position in the news media meant that he could help bring about changes in established orders. It was not a new role for Jack; setting the record straight and recording events accurately were essential to him. It was not only a duty to do such but a sacred right. This was a lesson Jack had learned early in life, not only in Hebrew school but in his public school and the whole neighborhood of the Grand Concourse.

Jack loved those things as nothing else. From his family's apartment on 167th Street you could look south and see most of Manhattan. Roosevelt Island was visible and you could see the tresseled towers of the Williamsburg Bridge. You could easily see the spirals of the Empire State and Chrysler Buildings and the lazy haze that Jersey spilled above the Hudson River. His friends, the Epsteins, lived on the northeast corner of the building; all they could see were miles and miles of the Bronx, brick, concrete and an occasional tree.

Within six blocks of the apartment, they had everything they needed. At school Jack had the best teachers; each year his same section advancing with the same friends. In the first section (6-1) of the sixth grade the only kid who was not one of "the tribe" was Al Wong. It was the elite "#1" class that took regular field trips and had all the cultural advantages. By the time Jack had reached junior high school, he had been to every museum, conservatory, exhibit, public building, monument, garden, library and college in New York City. This was his home and it had everything he wanted or needed; the right foods, theater, concert, art, people and culture.

Later he and his friends crisscrossed the city by subway. They went everywhere that was "safe." Some subway stops were for "others." The train would have to slow down, stop, open and close the doors, and then gradually accelerate back to cruising speed.

Two afternoons a week during the school year there were 90 minutes of Hebrew school. Once the right to left magic of reading Hebrew was mastered, the later grades moved onto debates over the Mishnah and Talmud, discussions of Torah and Kashrut. On long subway rides, Jack would go over the Hebrew laws in his mind. By heart he could recite the ten commandments not only forward but backwards in Hebrew and in English.

One summer he went to camp up in the Catskills, north of West Point. They left on a Thursday and it was an hour's boat ride up the Hudson to New Rochelle. From New Rochelle they took the bus to the camp. They shared their two weeks with a group of boys from Williamsburg in Brooklyn. Those boys were even more orthodox than Jack's group. They wore their yarmulkes all the time, the tzizis every day beneath their shirts; they all had their hair locked with payes; countless discussions; what constitutes white for the tachrichin; what is a true cloven foot; which fish may be eaten. The two groups in endless discourse—could you dance on the Sabbath; was it right to travel when you were sick; could you immerse the mikvah on the Sabbath; how many of the mitzvoth are positive (248); name the sections of Shulhan Arukh; and on and on, endless!

Jack admired the boys from Brooklyn. They had a difficult and rigid life but they knew the law in its entirety. They knew the restric-

71

tions that were placed in dealing with one's neighbors and what price was imposed for improper conduct. When Jack left camp that summer, he felt a greater enrichment. He was part of a tradition that was as old as time itself. Its laws, customs, and rights down to this day preserved not only on tablets and papers but in hearts never to be erased.

These weren't the only things in New York that were a part of Jack though. The parks and Yankees he loved, and visits to them with his friends he still cherished. But it was the libraries that he loved the most. One summer he read the entire Jewish encyclopedia. By the time he entered high school, he had read the works of Fast, Bellow, Green and Spinoza. By the time he had finished high school he had read Michener, Hecht, Mocher, and Dukes. He had also plotted the stars from the Hayden Planetarium and read the works of Cohen and Del Medigo. Only the Yankees and Dodgers distracted him from his quest for knowledge. But even with those, he computed who gave up the most home runs in winning and losing ball games; who had the most strikeouts with men on base; who had thrown the most wild pitches with two men out; how many Yankees had there been who had three "s's" in their name.

When high school came Jack was easily placed in Bronx Science. He devoured math and chemistry, A's in physics and biology, and he won an award in the city science fair. But it was words that keep coming back to Jack; words, definitions, grammar, sentences, and paragraphs. By the time he had reached the 10th grade, he knew what he wanted to do. He had watched Columbia University since he was twelve years old. He had studied its architecture, he had run across the field where the great Yankee, Lou Gehrig, had played. He had seen the library at night, lit up by billions of excited photons generating energy. Although he had walked through the campus many, many times, he had never gone into the library. He had decided he would save that for a later time when he would be a student. Jack collected A's in high school like some kids collect sports trophies or like a mason bricks, for laying in a walkway. Each prize and award lead closer and closer to the Emerald City. He would never leave New York! When Jack finished Bronx Science, most of his friends went to CCNY and Jack entered Columbia's School of Journalism after finishing second in his graduating high school class.

When Jack came to Tallawampa it was only his second trip to

Dixie —the first had been to Miami with his parents. On the way back driving through Georgia, they couldn't get a motel room on the interstate. Rather than go off the main road they drove all night. For some reason, he was very conscious of his Jewishness in the south. He had been to Europe twice and in spite of all its problems and history he felt perfectly safe there. In Europe Jack was an American and didn't worry about going anywhere, but here in Dixie it was different. He was an American dealing with Americans, yet it was different. But no matter, justice was justice and he was going to see that it was done. Maybe these people would get out of the noose this time, but if they did they wouldn't the next time; and if they did, at some point there would be an end to it.

Jack reported his findings in Tallawampa and his meetings with John Prichard to the Times. Each new meeting between the two men was begun with a new resolve. Prichard would give an inch and he would then dodge behind the same legalisms. Another day John interrupted the interview.

"You said last week Genghis Khan was a Tartar. He wasn't; he was a Mongol."

"No, no, he was a Tartar. Actually a Tartar is one of the many Mongolian peoples." It was a genuine time out from their business and both men knew it. Jack just knew that Prichard was going to get away with this. Though this infuriated Jack, there was a politeness that came from John Prichard; he was pleasant, mannered and never offended; for this Jack had admiration.

If Jack Farakshnt and the other newsmen were disappointed about the information they received from John, they were even more disappointed by the townspeople. The local people held back in total caution. Pleasant and polite, but extremely cautious. "The conspiracy," the newsmen dubbed it.

The T.V. people had focused on the courthouse. They were there with their cameras and lights multiple times throughout the day. They would shoot a scene from various angles and with different people only to return several hours later to do the same thing over again.

Some of the reporters went to the various offices in the courthouse—the land records and even the selective service records. "They're probably looking to see if Brooks has ever been in the Army," speculated someone.

Tallawampa made the national television news twice before the trial. Both times there was a man with a slight, though not a local, southern accent standing in front of Tallawampa's courthouse, the beautiful building draped with its trees and shaded lawn as a backdrop. The first time he began, "This is a peaceful, quiet community deep in Alabama, but peaceful nor quiet is it always, or has it been. Last month a man was shot and murdered here. Murdered not for what he did but for what he was; like twenty million other Americans, he was black. It's happened before, the same thing. In the past, nothing has been done about such murders and it is the growing fear by many that nothing will be done again." In Tallawampa that night part of the town citizens gulped when they saw the newscast. The rest of the citizens just sat and watched with quiet resignation.

The second national T.V. appearance for Tallawampa was again from in front of the courthouse but from a different view. This presentation was part of a larger report on civil rights activities in general. By now the murder and trial were nearly household words. The reporter for this presentation was equally polished and again with a touch of a southern accent. Maybe from Tennessee, thought John, probably educated up north. The reporter began, "Next week a trial for murder begins here in Tallawampa, Alabama. The murder of Wardel Mackel at a church picnic. The state has moved fast to complete the trial of the accused. In fact, too fast some say. At least too fast for justice's sake. Punishment for first-degree murder in Alabama is death, but no one really believes that will happen to the defendant. But that doesn't mean people haven't been executed in Alabama before though. Why, one was hung right over there," as the camera zoomed in on the tree next to the jail. "He was hung for stealing chickens. He was also black." The town buzzed; the next day was filled with the news story. "I don't remember anyone being hung for stealing chickens."

"Either do I."

"It must have been an awful long time ago."

"Well, for God's sake, don't say anything to anybody; sure enough they'll come up with some record somewhere where there was someone hung for it."

"Call the attorney general's office and see if they have any records of anybody being hung for stealing chickens."

Two days after the second T.V. presentation the weekly news

74

magazine came out and Tallawampa made the front cover. The magazine article about the trial had a different effect. Once the T.V. news show was over the only way to remember it was by your own recall; but the magazine was right there with you for the whole week. You could reread it as many times as you were tempted and somehow you couldn't break away from the pictures. On the front cover of the magazine, there was a picture of a central explosion that divided the cover into four quadrants; in one of the quadrants there were some black kids running in the surf of a beach being chased by police. In the second quadrant there was a picture of police dogs attacking demonstrators; in the third, there were black youths picketing with posters in front of a bus station restaurant; in the last quadrant of the cover was a picture of Tallawampa's courthouse.

The lead article described the weekly civil rights events. Tallawampa was described as a tight-lipped, non-communicative community ruled by a small inner group. Judge Newbold was mentioned as a recluse. John was described as evasive and secretive. There was no mention of William Marmande. The article recalled the last execution in Tallawampa, 1927, when Willie Vaughn was hung at the county jail for robbery and murder. Since that time all executions in Alabama had been moved from the local counties to the state penitentiary.

The town had been tight-lipped all right. The Mayor had referred all parties to the prosecutor, John Prichard. John answered no one. The town's people didn't talk to anyone. They just kept on walking and doing what they were about; if they could hold out for just a few more weeks, the whole thing would be over.

Although Judge Newbold stayed on the farm, he had kept up with events. The Judge had evaluated his roll long before the shooting. In fact, before Wardel had even come to town.

This would not be Thomas Newbold's first murder trial. He had ruled on many murder trials and from those he had sent four men to their executions. Two of those men were the Field brothers, who, after breaking into the home of farmer George Murtough, robbed the man and then proceeded to kill him. They then murdered the dead man's wife after abusing her in a most vile way. When the Murtough's two daughters, Becky and Lynn, ages ten and eleven, returned from a 4-H meeting and interrupted the intruders, they were promptly shot by the two thugs. For those acts the Field brothers sat grissled in Kilby State Penitentiary before the new moon. The third man sent to his execution by Thomas Newbold was Copen Taylor who, because of a domestic quarrel, set his neighbor's house on fire then shot the neighbor when he fled the inferno as the flames enveloped the man's common law wife and two children. The fourth person sent to the same end was William E. Butler. William E. had robbed the seventy-four year old postmistress at the rural retreat of Shadyside of $28.40. William then proceeded to fracture the old woman's skull. Thomas Newbold had no trouble meting out justice.

Thomas was ready for this trial. He had reviewed the criminal statutes of the state as well as the rules of evidence and procedures. There were going to be no stains on Thomas Newbold's courtoom from Tallawampa or from afar.

Thomas had been on the bench of the Circuit Court of his native county for nearly ten years. He had grown up at Somerset just west of Tallawampa. There had been Newbolds there for as long as anyone could remember. Parts of the original farm or plantation had been sold over the years piece by piece, but the main house and buildings, as well as the adjoining two hundred forty acres, were still intact. These were the acres Thomas farmed as a boy with his father, and they are the same acres he farms today. He was the oldest of the five children and this placed him in a position of responsibility and trust early in life. It was a position he accepted seriously. Even in his earliest years he marshalled the others into place and parcelled out the various works needed to be done. His memories of Somerset go back before Francis, his younger brother, was born. Mother about the house; she was awake before he arose in the morning and was awake when he went to bed at night. She was continuously moving, doing, working, sewing, mending, cleaning, getting eggs, washing; not frenzied activity but constant and steady. The kitchen, the children's rooms and the washroom—those were her world. And when mother became pregnant with Francis, their parents told the unsuspecting children that they had a surprise. With the announcement of the expected child there was great glee; little Catherine mooned her eyes and held her ears. The following months were in great anticipation. They watched mother go about the house with the same chores and same tasks. with a growing fatigue and faint anxiety.

Finally, one day his father dashed upstairs and hurried into Thomas' room. "Thomas, stay with your mother, do as she says,"

His father raced away in search of help. Thomas went to his mother's room; she was in bed, bloated turning her torso from one side to the other, extending one leg and then the other beneath the blanket.

"Thomas, stay in the kitchen with the girls." Thomas marshalled Margaret, Catherine and Mary Ann into the kitchen. The two younger girls began to cry. They could hear mother upstairs. Then someone was at the door; it was dad and Moses' Ufala. The two adults rushed upstairs.

"Mr. Thomas, you wait downstairs. You children, put some water on and get me some towels." A pot on each burner in an instant; towels of all sizes, shapes and colors were collected from flights to rooms in the house. They were piled on mother's bed. "You children, go downstairs," Ufala told them with assurance. Father and children in the kitchen waiting; before long they heard the child; father was instructed to come up and take the baby. Dad returned with the infant and held him in front of the others, all in awe.

Ufala stayed upstairs with mother. Fifteen minutes, a half an hour, then an hour. She instructed them all to stay downstairs. It would be only a few more moments. The afterbirth, it just wouldn't come. There was tugging and pulling and more tugging and more pulling until finally it too was delivered. Mother rested that day, tired and exhausted. There was a quiet party in the kitchen that evening. The four children with their new sibling, dad, and Ufala. Mrs. Smarr and Mrs. Nelson, neighbors' wives, also came by. The following day mother stayed in bed, weak and without appetite. It was a soreness in her abdomen. particularly in the lower part that kept her there: by the end of the second day the soreness had developed into pain. On the morning of the third postpartum day, the pain was severe. Mother lay in bed drenched with perspiration. That evening they rushed her to Montgomery to the hospital; but the infection was too great and she died that night. The baby was placed in the care of Ufala, and God bless that poor old lady's soul for she nursed and tended Francis as if he were her own.

The family stayed on the farm, the children and Thomas' father, as he grew older Thomas assumed more responsiblity. He frequently put the children to bed to complete his own chores. He and the others worked the fields with their dad with hand and hoe. They used sharecroppers and tractor only when needed. They planted everything they had and harvested much less. They extracted what they could from the soil, depleted of its former black richness, eroded by rains and partially filled with blight. For some reason the land always seemed parched. When the rain fell it all came in one day and, in fact, in less than an hour. There would be such a downpour as to wash away the top soil leaving nothing but diatones of clay. Then there would be no rain for another month. Scrawny little shoots of crops standing in earth more and more composed of clay. They would drive to the river in a caravan, the tractor first, pulling the largest wagon, and then the mules pulling the flatbeds. There they would load milkcans with water from the river and return to the fields. They would rise long before daybreak so that the water would not evaporate and the plants would have the greatest benefit to absorb the nutrient before being evaporated by the heat of day. They would return to the river sometimes two and three times in a day and ladle the precious water on to the withered seedlings. Each day they renewed the venture. One day the axle broke on the wagon and another day they lost two of the cans in the river. Those latter two when they filled with water rapidly sank. The clutch of the tractor broke and after it was repaired the valve on the carburetor failed. They stood there in the field, Thomas with his siblings, and his father with the ebony fieldhands assembled around the heavy cans beginning their journey down the rows of plants; seedlings barely out of the ground and up to their ankles in July. By the time they finished a row the beginning plants would be surrounded by the same parched mud. Thomas saw his father's disappointment. "Don't worry, daddy, when we have our crop everything will be all right."

His father looked away and hid his face; he wept and told Thomas, "There's not going to be a crop, Thomas, there's not going to be anything."

"Sure there will be daddy." But Thomas stopped himself and his father continued.

"Jesus, Thomas don't go out in that field unless you have a hat on."

He watched the tears run down his father's face. "But I wear a hat daddy," he whispered back.

"I don't mean a hat on your head, Thomas, you go as far in that school as you can go and don't you stop until there's no more." His father paused. "You run along now, Thomas, you go on to the house with the other children and see if you can't fix something for

78

dinner." Thomas left with the others and went to the house; from there he watched his father walking down the rows of plants examining each, measuring some and rationing water to each step by step, draft by draft.

But if those were hard times, there was food and they had the cow. They had the chickens and the rooster, too; and woe to any fox that went near them. They had the garden, and both Margaret and Catherine were becoming good with skillet and pan, and little Mary Ann was beginning to sew. Soon Francis was able to chop wood and gather eggs. Each evening they talked, they read, and they comforted one another. On Saturdays they went to town and on Sundays they went to church. Sometimes on Sundays they even went to Mellons for ice cream. The years passed and when it came time for Thomas to go to school, they drove to Tallawampa for Dr. Christy to drive Thomas to Tuscaloosa. The girls kissed their older brother and said their goodbyes; Thomas' father's parting words were goodbye and good luck. As Thomas and the doctor, serving as his chauffeur, drove off to take Thomas to college, he turned and watched his father standing there motionless and the children waving softly until he could see them no more.

After college and then law school, Thomas returned to Tallawampa and opened his law offices. It was only a short time thereafter that he ran for county office. There he protected the interest of his neighbors. His sisters married and left to form new homes; his younger brother, Francis, bought a farm in Creek. Finally, the Somerset farm was divided equally among the five children and Thomas bought each of the other's shares. With this he and his wife, Comfort, moved into the house where he had been born and lived. The house that had surrounded him with joys and sorrows and brought him to manhood.

Thomas and Comfort were married eleven years before Molly was born, and with her conception there was a thrill of expectation he had never known. The child would add completeness to their lives, and when Molly was born there was a joy that vibrated through the house and in both he and Comfort's lives. Delights never imagined; numbered blocks, crayoned circles, delicious gentle kisses, tattered limp dolls, secret hiding places, parties, one candle, then two and then a third, beautiful innocence! The child pulling at his sleeve in the evening as he lay on the couch, "Daddy, daddy, dinner time, dinner time." The first days of school when autumn came with its clear coolness and rain that drenched the earth, and the excitement of occasional flakes of snow. When Thomas went on to the bench they had a family portrait done—he, Comfort and Molly. But even with the ever increasing joys there was a slight apprehension and guardedness about Molly. There was something wrong. Molly didn't thrive quite as well as she should have. She had a paleness and her skin was slightly waxy. There were numerous episodes of bed wetting; Comfort and Thomas were told that this was unusual for little girls. Her urine had a peculiar darkness, and on occasions there was a puffiness about her eyes. On other days, her feet and hands were swollen.

Something was wrong; they knew it. They took Molly to Dr. Christy. He told them it was her kidneys. The two parents looked at each other in bewilderment; "Her kidneys," they asked out loud. "Why, there's no kidney disease in our families."

Dr. Christy told Thomas that it was serious. "How serious?" asked Comfort.

"The doctor didn't say, he just said that it was serious."

"What will we do?"

"I don't know. He says that the disease in the kidneys allows blood to come out in the urine."

"I've never heard of blood in someone's urine."

"Neither have I," answered Thomas.

They decided to take Molly to Minnesota for diagnosis and to see what could be done. They prepared for the trip not only as a venture to the hospital but also as a grand vacation. There was great secrecy and intimacy about the eight-year old Molly wearing a diaper. For the train ride they had brought a rubber sheet for Molly's mattress. They were gone almost two weeks and on the return trip home they stopped in St. Louis. They took the steam boat from there to Memphis. They had diagnosed the trouble as nephritis and somehow or other there had been an infection in Molly's throat that had poisoned and settled in her kidneys. The sore throat was precipitated by a bacteria associated with colds and sore throats. One of the doctors had asked about the colds and standing in the rain with wet feet; he had stated that this was a common association. When they returned home Thomas examined Molly's golashes for defects; he filled them with water to see if they were porous. He examined the brick

80

walkway in front of the house to see if there were puddles and he measured the depth of each. He surveyed the terrace of the lawn and measured the cavities there. He took loam and graded the earth. He measured the walkway again and graded the bricks. He stood in the rain himself to see how the puddles formed. But in spite of all these retroactive measures, Molly became progressively tired and her bed wetting increased as did her swelling. Finally, she dropped out of school, and Molly spent more and more time in bed. Comfort reading to her, the two spending the dwindling hours together. The parents consulted Dr. Christy again. "What is to be done?"

"There is nothing to be done."

"Where do we take her?"

"There is no place to take her, only home."

The swelling became progressive and now there were intermittent episodes of shortness of breath as the bed wetting became less frequent. Molly sat up in bed propped on one pillow, then on two as her shortness of breath and fluid retention became more severe. She died in her ninth year. Thomas held her that day, for how long he can't remember; the three of them in the little girl's room, finally Comfort's voice whispering softly, "Thomas, you have to let her go, Thomas, you have to let go."

"Yes," he responded distraught and resigned; he laid the child down. After Molly's funeral Thomas returned to the bench. He consumed his hours there and on the farm. In the courtroom he listened and ruled on the repetitive complaints of the participants. On the farm he filled his hours with rotations, fertilizers, aeration experiments and livestock, as well as his papers on the confederate judiciary. He studied and meticulously kept records of the Circuit Court during the civil war period—the terms of the court, rule days, judgments, writs, orders, and codes, most of which were retained with reunification of the states.

This passion for past causes instilled in Thomas a proper order and keen exactness for judicial proceedings. On the morning of the trial he arose early and went to the courthouse and his chambers long before anyone had assembled at the courthouse. There he thought about his previous murder trials and about the women and children who had been killed by the four men he had had executed. He stayed uninterrupted in his office until 9:30 when the Clerk nervously knocked on his door, "Judge, Judge, I think they're ready to start." When he walked into the room it was packed and all stood. Thomas stood in silence looking at the participants and the spectators; his pause continued. He knew everyone who was there or at least who they were; he continued standing in silence. There would be no nonsense in this room; Thomas sat down for the beginning of the trial.

Chapter Six

Thomas motioned for the clerk to hand him the list of prospective jurors. "Gentlemen," the Judge began looking at John and William Marmande, "You have the list of prospective jurors before you to examine before exercising a preemptory strike."

In a moment William Marmande began, "Your Honor, if it pleases the court, as I look down this list I see no one that I would want to strike. All of these people look very qualified, and I am happy to defend my case before any of these persons."

"Your Honor, I see no reason to strike any of the prospective jurors either and the state will be pleased to try its case with the jurors appointed by the court." John Prichard wasn't going to be outgentlemaned by William Marmande.

The clerk took the first twelve names on the list and informed the bailiff to instruct the twelve persons to take their seats in the jury box. Number eight on the list was Turpin Ellis. John had noticed Turpin's name first when he was handed the list. He either knew each person of the twelve or recognized their names. Turpin Ellis was the one that presented the greatest problem. Turpin was a hog farmer who, it is fair to say, liked no one (or if he did, nobody knew who it was). From that point of reference Turpin had a long list of people that he progressively disliked and there was one group of people who were way down on his list. Turpin would be John's common denominator. If John could reach Turpin, the others would be easy.

John watched as the jurors took their places and the bailiff administered the oath. There was Turpin in the middle of the first row, his sun-baked skin pulled so tight over his head that there was no room for an expression, just the deep wrinkles of tight skin pulling at the corners of his mouth.

With the jurors settled the Judge asked John if he was ready to begin. When John responded, "Yes," Thomas Newbold instructed him to do so. John's opening statement was brief and matter of fact, totally without emotion. There had been a murder—a raw, pointless murder. The defendant had committed the crime. The state had the murder weapon, the bullets, the fingerprints and could prove by expert witnesses the defendant's guilt. His opening statement was barely 20 minutes. William Marmande elected not to make an opening statement. The Judge then instructed John to call his first witness.

John rose, turned and looked around the packed room but wasn't able to find Jack Farakshnt in the crowd. He then turned to the Judge, "Your Honor, the state's first witness is Jeremiah Crowley." After the F.B.I. agent had been sworn in and properly identified to the court, John went through a series of questions of why and how Jeremiah Crowley came to be in Tallawampa.

The fair, blond agent responded in Ozarkian tones and explained the investigative nature of his work; how he and his agency often can see a predictable calamity approaching but how they are unable to prevent it; also, how being near the Mississippi border this was a possible location for violations in interestate commerce as kidnapping; that these matters were under his agency's jurisdiction. Crowley continued how, in the course of his investigations, they had become aware of Wardel Mackel and his activities in Tallawampa; also that Wardel was part of a group that spread across the south, and that his continued activity in Tallawampa alone made him particularly vulnerable to danger. John next led Crowley into the events of the murder and how he and his associate had found the body and how they had notified the sheriff. John had Crowley describe the events that Sunday morning up to the time that the prosecutor had arrived at Mt. Zion field. There was a harmony between the prosecutor and his witness that was apparent to everyone. If there were two Mr. Cleans in the courtroom that day, they were Jeremiah Crowley and John Prichard and everyone knew it. When Crowley ended his testimony of the events of the murder, John asked him two more questions.

"Mr. Crowley, did you know Wardel Mackel—I don't mean personally, but to talk to?"

"I never spoke to him but I observed him off and on for several months."

"And from what you know of him, how would you describe Wardel Mackel?"

Crowley deliberated for a moment and then said, "determined"—he repeated the word again, "determined."

When John indicated that he had no further questions, Judge Newbold looked to William Marmande. The defense lawyer rose and answered almost inaudibly. "No question, your Honor."

John's next witness was Sheriff Redtop. Redtop had his faults but he was well liked (elected three times), and he protected the citizens' property. He told the room at John's request the details of finding the dead victim and the arrest of Ross Brooks. He told about the four bullet wounds and how Mackel had run down the path. Redtop told the court about the gun and about the bullets that he had found in Ross Brooks' room; also how Ross had bragged about the shooting. Then John asked the Sheriff if anyone was with Brooks the night of the shooting. When the Sheriff responded that yes, there were three others with Brooks, John next asked the Sheriff to name the three.

"Dwayne Turner, John Trunkel, and Charles Pith."

Throughout the Sheriff's testimony, there was a slight amount of banter between the prosecutor and Redtop. The Sheriff was also mildly theatrical. He enjoyed being on the stand. He was in a no-lose situation and knew it. He had solved the case, disarmed the villain, apprehended the culprit, arrested the murderer and he kept him locked in the county jail. When he answered the questions he addressed the gallery as much as he did John. He couldn't be held responsible for what the court did or didn't do with Ross Brooks. The Sheriff displayed his police work the best he could to the voters. John was complementary to the Sheriff and it was again obvious that the two men were on good terms. When John concluded his questions, Judge Newbold again looked to the defense. Again the same response.

"No questions, your Honor."

At this point the Judge instructed the room, "We will continue after lunch, two P.M."

John waited in the courtroom after the recess was announced to

85

give the room a chance to clear out. He would go down Third Street and make it home for lunch, but before he was off the courthouse green there was Farakshnt.

"Determined! So that's it," began Farakshnt.

"Determined! Determined to get killed, is that it? Is that it Prichard? I swear Prichard, I've never seen anything so low. What could that poor freak Brooks do but shoot him; and the Sheriff, my, my, old pals around the courthouse. Just some good old boys having a good time. Why didn't you ask about the fingerprints? Why didn't you ask him about the ballistics? Why didn't you ask what the three men saw out there instead of just who was with Brooks that night? Why didn't you ask him that, Prichard?" his voice rising with rage and indignation. "Why didn't you ask them that?"

"It's only the first day," John began.

"Only the first day," interrupted Farakshnt. "You bet it's only the first day, but I have news for you, friend, it's also the third century and before we're finished we'll turn this place upside down and inside out; and if you don't believe me, you'll see." Jack left in a furor.

John was relieved when he arrived home for lunch. He told Jenny about his two witnesses. He also told her about Turpin Ellis. "Boy, if I can crack that old nut I can do anything." But John was down; he told Jenny about Farakshnt and his remarks on the courthouse lawn.

She reassured John, "I'm sure you did fine. You could hardly prosecute your case without calling those two men as witnesses; and they were the first two men involved with the murder; seems logical to me that you should call them first; and why shouldn't they be your friends—you'd hardly want them to be your enemies."

Her kind words lightened this load. He described the other jurors to Jenny as well as Judge Newbold. "William Marmande didn't have a question for either witness; just stood there and let their testimony lay, no objections at all." He described others in the courtroom to Jenny so she could give her free-lance opinions and recommendations. He described Ross to Jenny as well. "He didn't seem remorseful, maybe regretful, that it wasn't worth all the trouble."

A few minutes before two John took his leave and returned to the courthouse. There was an easiness and lightness as the afternoon session began. Nobody was going to get stuck with a dagger and nobody was going to get blown away after all. Everybody could relax and could proceed with what they were about.

"Mister prosecutor, call your next witness," began Judge Newbold.

"Your Honor, the state's next witness is Doctor Newton Christy." When he announced the doctor's name, the whole room was still as the aging but active physician went to the stand. There wasn't a person in Tallawampa that hadn't had the healing ways of Dr. Christy. They would all listen to him.

"Doctor, could you," began John, "tell the jury what you know about the death of Wardel Mackel?" The Doctor began with his phone conversation with John about the body being found and then about the events of the autopsy. How they had examined the body and how they determined the sequence of the fired bullets. He described the wounds to the leg, chest and head. After he had described these he explained the bases for his conclusions. When the Doctor finished, John continued with another question.

"Doctor, wasn't Wardel Mackel shot a fourth time, that is, twice to the head, and weren't both these wounds inflicted after he was dead."

"Yes, they were," responded the Doctor.

"Is there a name for that, Doctor, inflicting injury to someone who is already dead?"

"Necrovilification, it's called."

"What does it mean, that is, what does necrovilification signify in a person? Who does such a thing, Doctor?"

"Great rage and hatred of your supposed adversary. A rage and hatred so great that it could not have been caused by anything the victim could have done. It is a pitiful state."

John paused and let the Doctor's words settle into the room. Then he continued, "Doctor, the murder weapon was found some 60 feet from where Wardel Mackel's body was, in a wooded area. It was thrown in the air from where Wardel Mackel lay. Can you place any significance on this—why the murder weapon is thrown in the air like this?"

"It usually signifies an act of jubilation, of triumph, an act that signifies accomplishment and achievement."

"You mean like a football player throwing the ball into the stands after he has scored a touchdown."

"Yes, something like that, yes."

87

John took just the briefest glance at the jury. Before the Judge could ask, William Marmande stood and in a murmur stated, "No questions, your Honor."

That's three I have on my side John thought to himself as the Doctor left the stand.

"Your Honor, if I may," John began and hesitated. The Judge motioned for him to continue. "I have another witness I can put on this afternoon or if it pleases the court, I can wait till tomorrow morning."

The Judge looked at William Marmande. "Tomorrow will be fine, Your Honor," obviously having had enough for one day.

"So be it, we are adjourned till tomorrow morning at 9:30."

"All rise," and the courtroom was cleared in a moment.

The next morning the courtroom was again filled to capacity. After introductory judicial formalities, John called his next witness, Mr. Raymond Leeder of the Alabama State Laboratories. Mr. Leeder was in charge of the state criminal laboratory in Montgomery. It was Mr. Leeder and his staff who had examined the pistol and the bullets for both fingerprints and ballistics.

Mr. Leeder, at John's request, described the fingerprints on the gun. He methodically described the characters produced by the papillary ridges of the skin on the hands, their arches, curves and contours, which were necessary to identify an individual's prints; he went into ulnar and radial loops and sizes of pattern areas. "Yes, the prints on the gun were Ross Brooks'. They were on the handle of the gun as well as the barrel and the chamber."

"And to what did you compare the fingerprints that you found on the gun?"

"I compared them to a set of fingerprints taken here in Tallawampa that your sheriff took from the defendant. I also compared them with a set of fingerprints that we obtained from the Tennessee State Penitentiary. There was a picture of the defendant that accompanied both sets of prints that were sent to us. The set on the gun, those from Tennessee and those from Sheriff Redtop are all the same person."

"The defendant there?" John asked motioning to Ross but without looking at him.

"Yes," responded Mr. Leeder.

"Mr. Leeder, the four bullets given to you by Sheriff Redtop, were those bullets fired by the same gun as the fingerprinted gun?" "Yes, they were. When a bullet travels down the barrel of a gun the imperfections on the inner lining of the barrel make marks on the passing bullet. These marks are characteristic of the gun. Also, the firing pin of a gun is just a little different from the firing pin of other guns. When the firing pin hits the casing of the shell when the trigger is pulled, the mark left on the casing is frequently characteristic of that gun. This mark is not always discernable even with a microscope but in this case it was." "The gun you examined then, Mr Leeder, the gun with Ross Brooks' fingerprints, that gun is the murder weapon, is that right?" "Yes. I have pictures of the bullets and the casings both with their markings that I can show you if you like."

William Marmande indicated no objection and John proceeded to introduce the photographs into evidence. On the photos were arrows that pointed out the significant strikes and angles. The photographs were passed to the Judge, jury, defense counsel, defendant and the clerk. The people in the seats near the participants strained their necks to see the exhibits. "Hum, they can really tell—well, I'll be." These photographs and Mr. Leeder's discussion were a new scientific high for Tallawampa.

When John was finished questioning Mr. Leeder, William Marmande examined his first witness. They were almost irrelevant questions and never contentious or challenging. Most of them really had little meaning to the case. "Just because Ross Brooks' fingerprints were found on the gun doesn't necessarily mean his hand was on the trigger when the fatal bullet was fired, does it, Mr. Leeder?"

"No, it doesn't," responded Raymond Leeder. That question and answer may have meant something but it was doubtful. John made no objections to any of William's questions. William must have gone on for 45 minutes or more asking questions about the markings on the bullets and the logistical relationship of the state laboratory with other agencies. He was pleasant to Mr. Leeder, maybe even ingratiating. Finally, at 11:30 William turned to the Judge, "Your Honor, I have no further questions of the witness."

Judge Newbold looked at the clock and then at the crowded gallery. "I think we'll break for lunch, court is adjourned till 1:30."

Jack Farakshnt had seen what he thought he was stalling tactics by William Marmande; some others suspected the same including John, but John was not concerned. He had one more witness to call, and he would just as soon let his last witness have the whole afternoon so that his testimony could sink in. He welcomed the breather before he started with his final witness.

Farakshnt caught John outside on the courthouse lawn during the adjournment, in fact, he had been waiting for him there. "I'm sorry about yesterday, Prichard, but I swear I don't get you," Jack began subdued. "Sometimes you come across as having it all together, then other times you're the worst of the lot. You can still prove your case if you call those witnesses," Jack implored.

John interrupted, "Jack, listen, everybody knows what happened out there that night. You know, I know, everybody knows. Why prove something they all know. My job is to get them to do something about it and I think I can." The two men parted.

After the noon recess there was quibbling in the gallery over who was sitting in whose seat. "I was there, that's my seat." This continued even when the clerk announced for all to rise. With the Judge's entrance the noise stopped, and when Thomas decided there was proper order he motioned for John to begin.

"Your Honor, I would like to call as my next witness, Charles Pith."

"What is this?" everyone in the courtroom asked themselves, "Charles Pith!" They all looked around the room to see if Charles Pith was actually present. Then they saw him rise from the back row and start for the witness stand.

Since the murder everyone in Tallawampa knew who Charles Pith was; before the murder he had been seen and dreaded so much that no one ever mentioned him. When it became known that there were three boys with Ross that night, there was a scurry by the townspeople to find out the names and link them with faces. When Charles Pith's name came up, "Oh, him. Well, I just think I'll stay home today and won't go out at all, Helen. I've been feeling sort of tired and I have so much to do."

"Why, why, he doesn't scare me none. I'll, I'll just call Sheriff Redtop. That's what we 'lected him for anyway. He won't come in here," the men had said as they glanced out the windows.

If Ross was the Provost of his group then Charles Pith had to be the bottom. Charles had to have some redeeming qualities for he had some friends. It was not that Charles Pith was so hostile or mean, or that he was unkempt, all of which he was; it was that he

90

was so threatening. It was easy to move out of the way when you saw Charles coming. It was the threatening eye contact that gave Charles Pith such an intimidating personality. But it was that with his other traits, together with his appearance, that made Charles just what he wanted to be. He loved it—the boots, black jacket and metal bracelet were symbols he wore with pride.

"Young man, you'll have to remove those glasses while you're on the witness stand," the Judge announced.

Charles removed his sunglasses as instructed without looking at the Judge. He glared at the people in the room—I'll show you bastards something—was clear to them all. He was obviously not afraid of anything or anybody and that he held John in contempt.

When the clerk nervously handed the Bible to Charles, he looked at it, then held it with both hands. When asked to state his name for the record, he said, "Charles Pith!" He looked around the room as he said his name. Who wants to challenge that, he glared. No one came forward. Charles Pith wasn't going to take on John Prichard; he was going to take on the whole courthouse.

Jack Farakshnt watched Charles from the back of the room in puzzlement. Many of the spectators looked the other way from Charles hoping that if their eyes didn't meet he would not know they were there.

Before John began with his questions of Charles, he positioned himself in front of the jury box, then walked slowly back and forth in front of the jurors. John would pause at each end of the juror's box; each pause became a little longer. Finally John began.

"Mr. Pith, do you live in Tallawampa?" he asked softly.

Charles tilted his head back with a snear indicating a yes. Before John could instruct him to verbalize his answer for the court reporter, the reporter nervously interjected that he saw the nod and recorded it as an affirmative answer.

"I have it, I have it."

"And how long have you lived in Tallawampa Mr. Pith?" John continued.

"I've lived here four years." Charles breathed with his mouth open. There was a slight hissing sound when he breathed in. His expirations were also audible.

"Where do you live in Tallawampa, Mr. Pith?" John was standing with his back to the jurors facing Charles.

91

"I live at Route 24 and 1st Street." Charles was impatient with such trivia and wanted to get to the heart of the matter. He was also suspicious for hidden meanings to John's questions.

"And you live there with friends, is that right?"

"That's right." What's it to you, came across.

"And Ross Brooks is one of your friends, is that right?"

"Yea, that's right," emphatically.

John then went into details about Ross' 1952 black Ford car; who used it, for what and where did they go; he asked about the episodes of taunting Wardel. Pith bragged about some of the incidents and also lied about others. They were unnecessary lies. John glanced over these. John established Charles and Ross as friends and even had Charles volunteer as a character reference for Ross. John still didn't mention the murder and Charles was growing more impatient.

"And what about a gun, did Ross Brooks have a gun?"

"Na, Ross didn't have any gun. Ross never had no gun!" More lies.

"And bullets?"

"No, he didn't have any bullets either. What he'd want bullets for if he didn't have a gun?"

Then finally, "You didn't see Ross Brooks shoot Wardel Mackel?"

"I didn't see nothin". I saw Ross hit some smart aleck on the head, and he deserved it too; shootin' off his big mouth, telling everybody what to do.

"At Mount Zion field, after the picnic that night, didn't you see Ross Brooks shoot Wardel Mackel?"

"Didn't I just tell you no? I saw him hit him on the head." Charles had tattooed on nine fingers a letter so that when he interlocked the fingers of his two hands the letters spelled a common vulgarity. At this point, as John stood in front of the jurors' box, Charles flashed the interlocking digital obscenity at John. This was as much physical hositility as Charles could get away with in a courtroom.

By now Charles had contradicted himself numerous times about the car, the gun, the incidents and the night of the murder. The contradictions were apparent and no one made any effort to correct them. After John was confident that everybody recognized the lies and contradictions, he looked at the jury pensively, then turned to

Charles. "And you stand by your friend, you insist he is innocent?" "That's right!" responded Charles. Charles had been on the witness stand for a little over an hour. When John finished his questions, William Marmande was asked if he had any cross examination. William shook his head 'no' without rising from his chair with his eyes lowered. William Marmande wanted no part of Charles Pith.

"If there are no other questions, then I think we have had enough for one day," the Judge hesitated. "I would like to thank everyone for their patience and participation so far in this case." He rose a little red-faced and exited.

John reviewed his day in court that evening with Jenny. He was out of witnesses now. He analyzed each witness' answers and re-evaluated his questions. The Doctor and Charles Pith were his best two, he thought. There is no way that Ross Brooks is going to get past the Doctor, John told Jenny. "And I was able to get Charles Pith to say just about anything I wanted him to say. I tied Brooks as tight as I could to Charles Pith. I don't know what else I could have done, all the witnesses came out good for me. I'm not sure who William Marmande will put on as witnesses. I can't believe he'll put on those other two fellows who were there with Ross that night. Maybe he won't put on anybody," continued John. "I could have come down harder on," as he continued his self analysis.

"I'm sure you did fine," assured Jenny. "Look good and evil, you're a natural winner."

"Yea," gulped John. "Well, now all I have is my summation, which ought to do it."

The next morning as John had anticipated, William Marmande had no witnesses to call, so his case would all be on his last and only statement.

"Since the defense elects to put on no witnesses, Mr. Prichard, are you ready for your summation?"

"I am, your Honor." John stole another glance at Turpin Ellis. John stood in front of the Judge's bench for a moment collecting his thoughts, the country boy mustering his persuasions together before the Judge and jury.

He began, "Your Honor, ladies and gentlemen of the jury. We have before us today a simple decision. One that we can reach without malice or scorn, without vindication or triumph. A simple decision of whether we do what is right and fair, and whether we have

93

compassion for those who have suffered."

"We have heard how a man has been murdered. Shot in the back while trying to seek refuge, while trying to escape his assailant. Not shot once but multiple times, shot until there was total lifelessness." He paused, "But what we must decide is why Wardel Mackel was shot and murdered. We have to determine the motive for his killing. Certainly Wardel was not killed for the usual reasons. Wardel Mackel was not killed because he was a thief, not because he was a rapist, not because he was himself a murderer, not because he was a criminal, not even because he was ill-mannered and not even because he had insulted his assailant. None of these reasons. Wardel Mackel was shot because he was black!" He waited again, "There has never been a law that says you can't be black; there has never been a statute that says it's a crime to be colored, but this is why Wardel was murdered." John waited again and then continued. "Wardel had nothing his assailant wanted. He had no money, no possessions, not even a watch. No valuables at all. Wardel's murderer wanted one thing and one thing only—his life and that only because Wardel was black. To rob, to maim, to steal, to kill—all these things are on the criminal codes as violations. Had Wardel done any of these things he would have been guilty of something, but there is no guilt in what he was." John turned and walked in front of the Judge, faced the jurors and continued. "What the defendant doesn't understand though is, if black is justification for murder, so is white; and if you can kill someone because of the color of their skin, you can also kill them for the color of their eyes. You are then justified in killing someone because they have red lips, cold hands, a frown, even a pleasant smile, or even a warm heart. If we accept the defendant's premise for murder we must accept the others as well. If this be the case, none of us are safe. We are all subject to the whims of villains. We all live in fear."

John stopped and rested. He had both hands on the railing of the jury box. He looked at each member. He shook his head negatively. He repeated the action. "Oh, no," he finally said. "Oh, no," he repeated, "that is not the only reason that Wardel Mackel was murdered. Umm, um, that's not the only reason, not just because he was black. He was murdered because his assailant is a coward. Yes, a coward," he whispered for emphasis. "He bragged about shooting Wardel! He bragged about shooting a defenseless person. He bragged about emptying his gun into a lifeless body. And then threw the gun in the air in jubilation. He didn't hide in guilt or despair but the defendant returned to his citadel of friends, proud and exhalted. Why did he do this?" John asked sharply. "Why does he brag, why does he exhalt himself after such an act?" He paused again and whispered to the still room, "I'll tell you why he does, I'll tell you why. Because he is so cock sure of himself. Because he is white. Because he is white," John repeated, "and he thinks because we are white that we will help him: that we will give him sanction and refuge in his crime; that we will protect him. In fact, because he thinks he has immunity, that he can kill that boy without being punished! And, that in some circles, he will even be a hero."

John walked away from the jurors, then reapproached them continuing, "Note that he is not only a coward but that he is also presumptive; presumptive that we will join in his crime, that we also will take some of the responsibility by not placing sanctions against him." He waited a full minute before he continued. "I believe this is a fatal mistake the defendant has made. I believe he has underestimated us and our character; and I think that this flaw in his judgment will cost him dearly!"

"We have heard much lately about justice in Alabama, or should I say, the lack of it. We have been told that we have never convicted one of us for such a crime as we have here. We have been held in front of the nation as being unjust. This alleged defect has been promulgated to everyone and now they all turn to look at us again. They wait to see what we will do, they wait for our display of character. They wait to see if we will slip into the quagmire with the defendant and partake in his crime. They wait to see if we will be as cowardly and as cruel as the defendant was." After a moment John went on with indignation, "But I say to you, we are just, we are fair, we are not afraid of what is right, we will do our duty! It is our place to find Ross Brooks guilty or innocent and we know which he is. The Judge can impart on him what sentence he thinks is fair but we must do our part. Ross Brooks, guilty; guilty as known—guilty as proven!"

John walked to his desk and took a bible from his briefcase. He turned to the passage he had marked from Dora's bible concordance. "I would like to read to you an excerpt from scripture.

'And on seeing the multitude, he went up into the mountains and he opened his mouth to teach them, saying,

95

Blessed are the poor in spirit, for theirs is the kingdom of the heavens. Blessed are they that mourn, for they shall be comforted. Blessed are they that hunger and thirst after justice for they shall have their fill. Blessed are they that have suffered persecution for justice sake, for theirs is the kingdom of heaven. For I tell you unless your justice abounds beyond that of the scribes and pharisees, ye shall not enter the kingdom of heaven. You have been told thou shall not kill and whoever killeth shall be liable to judgment.' "

When he finished, there was not a sound in the room, not even the fan overhead dared to make a noise. But everyone in the room was saying the same thing to themselves, "Hooray for our side."

After several moments, Judge Newbold looked at William, "I would like a recess, your Honor, if that is permissible?" John consented without speaking.

"A one-hour recess would take us to lunch time, shall we reconvene at 1 P.M.?" Thomas Newbold asked the two lawyers. Both agreed. With the sound of the gavel the room broke into noise and laughter—"whowees" and "boy, did he give it to em," could be heard. Numerous people came over and congratulated John; some just gave him a little tug on his coat sleeve without saying anything. Others just grinned and smiled. Dewey Bishop came over and just said, "Yep," a couple of times and that emptied out Dewey's heart.

When John made it through the crowd to the outside, Jack Farakshnt came running over to him. "Jesus, I can't believe it," Jack exclaimed. "I can't believe it, Jesus, you were great, Prichard, great! I'd have never thought it, and I've been set up besides. Wow!"

John embarrassed, thanked Jack for the praise. "You did it, you did, wow," repeated Jack.

"It's not over yet," John added.

"It's over all right! It's over. I saw you watching that old geezer in the front row. You had him eating out of your hands. It's over and I'm not finished yet, either!" John thanked his friend again as Jack dashed off.

John was exhausted. He walked down to Semmes Street but instead of going home he turned and went to the river to the abandoned wharfs. He couldn't wait until the trial began again. He was anxious to get it over. If the response that Jack and the crowd gave him were any sign of what the jury was going to do, he did have it. He was confident but there was the doubt. William Marmande hadn't said anything. A few perfunctory questions to the only out-of-town witness. John had presented all his evidence and now had given his psychological appeal. Everyone now saw John's hand, including William Marmande. Everything on the summation for William! John had stayed on the high ground throughout. Maybe William Marmande could turn Ross Brooks into a saint; no way for that, thought John. He passed along the riverfront till it was time for court to reconvene.

At one o'clock all were in the courtroom—the final round. Everyone had played their cards but William Marmande and now he was getting his one and only shot. All waited with eagerness.

William began, "Your Honor, members of the jury. All of us here in this room are interested in but one single thing; and the one thing is justice. We should seek no more and be satisfied with no less, that one quality, justice." John could feel the perspiration on his back. "Justice as we would ask for ourselves, for our friends and for others. Justice that ought not know any color, nor boundaries, nor any distinctions. Justice that is clear and justice that is straight. If we do that, if we can stand before ourselves and others with that in hand, we can stand with confidence and pride. If we fail, if we fail, we will carry the shame forever!" Oh, my lord, thought John, what's going on? "Let's examine closely what we have before us," continued William. "Let us find where the villain's hands lie. Let us search the road that has brought us here, and let's be fair and equal to all. We have been told that Wardel Mackel was not killed for money, not killed for revenge, but because he was black, and it is true—but who has made black the enemy," he asked sharply. "Not this boy," pointing to Ross. "He sets no standards for society. He abides by society's rules and if he does not, he is punished. Oh, no, not him, he sets no standards. Ross Brooks is like Wardel Mackel; he is a small part of society, at the edge. Ross Brooks like Wardel Mackel has acted out the role that each has been given. He has responded in a way many of us had anticipated and anticipated by many others not in this room. In fact, he has done what some have covertly hoped he would do. And, alas, by this he has fallen into a trap. He has taken the bait with some faulty notion of valor, of imaginary victory, but he is marked forever. Now that he is caught by his dreadful deed, those who have tricked him call for vengeance. Why should their passion for retribution be satisfied. Why should their passion for what they call justice be approved. Only one reason," added William nodding his head knowingly. "Only one reason—to relieve their guilt. Take notice, the deceased' family is not here. Wardel's friends are not here. It is not they who seek retribution; they are in sorrow, in grief with their loss. They mourn their loved one. They sit in prayer. If they ask for anything at all, it is not for more blood but for the end of it. But who are these provocators who prey upon society, who hide behind unseen walls, who call for retribution, who tempt the unknowing into dangerous and shameful acts. These same people tell us we have never convicted anyone of what the defendant did. What they says is true, we have not!" William was now standing in front of John's desk facing the jury. "But what they have failed to tell you is neither has our sister state, Mississippi, executed a white man for the murder of a negro." He had begun tapping his knuckles lightly on John's desk. "They didn't tell you that. Nor has our other sister state, Georgia. No, they didn't tell you that either; and what they also forgot to tell us was neither has Tennessee or Kentucky. These same provocators also forgot to tell us that neither has Carolina or Virginia." He had increased his tapping on John's desk until it was a thumping. His voice was now in indignation. He began slowly approaching the jury with his eyes aflame. "Neither has Indiana or Illinois," he whispered. "Nor has Michigan or Wisconsin, nor Pennsylvania or New York, and neither have Rhode Island or Massachusetts. No, no," he screamed out. "Don't ask us to be punitive with one of ours, they say, it is you who must offer up the sacrifice to ease our guilt." His raised voice was trembling now. "I say to you, we are like the defendant. We are one of the lesser ones. Let those who exhault an eye for an eye, a tooth for a tooth, let them pluck their own eye, let them extract their own tooth and we shall follow. Let us not fall into the same trap these unfortunate boys did, and that somehow we will be exonerated if we but sacrifice one of ours."

"Justice!" William bellowed. "Justice! It is the law of the land! We ask no more and want no less." John turned slightly and found Jack Farakshnt in the gallery. He bit his lip and shook his head faintly. His moistened eyes told his thoughts. Jack stared back in disbelief.

98

William had now returned to his desk and he too produced a bible. He began, "I also would like to read a passage from scripture." He made no effort to wipe away the tear. "It is from the beloved John.

'They said to him, 'Master this woman hath been caught in the very act of adultery. Now Moses in the law commanded us to stone such. What do you say?' And this they said tempting him that they might have cause to accuse him. But Jesus stooped down and wrote with his finger in the sand. When they continued asking him he raised himself and said to them, 'Let him who is without sin among you cast the first stone.' And again he stooped down and wrote in the sand. But they, when they heard this, went away one by one beginning with the eldest; and when he was left alone—'"

William had to interrupt his reading. His voice quivered and broke. He had to stop again; these were real emotions from William Marmande and everyone knew it. He continued his reading,

"and he was left alone, and only the woman standing in his midst. Jesus raising himself said to her, 'Woman where are your accusers.' I have none, Lord, and Jesus responded, 'nor do I accuse you, go, sin no more.'"

The jury was out for only 40 minutes. When they returned, their verdict was "not guilty". John stood outside the courthouse with well wishers. Dewey Bishop came over and said hello; and there was Jack. The two men had started walking down the courthouse walkway when they heard, "John, John." It was William Marmande. He hurried to catch up with them. The two men congratulated each other. "Bill, do you know Jack Farakshnt?"

"I don't believe I've had the pleasure, sir!" Jack was disarmed by the warm hand and the sincere smile. "It's a hot day, let me treat you all to a Pepsi. Is Mellons all right, John? Will that be all right, Mr. Farakshnt?" asked William.

"Sure, sure, anything will be fine."

The three men walked to Mellons, ordered Pepsis and sat in the window; they traded tales and shared lightness. It was a relief to have this trial done and levity was easy to come by. They argued about the 45 cents check. William won because he had invited and was the oldest.

"You know, they say in West Virginia, that the older a bull gets the harder his horns are," said John.

"Well, it's not true in Alabama, at least not in Washington County." They laughed and hee heeed.

"You know why pessimists like German restaurants?" asked Jack.

"No."

"Because they always expect the worst; get it the wurst." The other two looked away shaking their heads laughing.

They talked about Florida, fishing, and investments. "Don't tell me about utilities," one moaned. At one point Jack asked William, "Are you sure about those states?" but he knew the answer before he had asked the question. They drained their cups. Suddenly, John noticed Jenny walking up First Street toward Mellons. It had been awhile since John had noticed how pretty Jenny was. He watched her as she approached, the breeze gently pressing her dress against her form. He left his friends and went outside. He stood there watching her approach, erect, smiling, always smiling. God, how does she do it. By now John had started walking toward her. She read his face to know his mood.

"Disappointed," she asked still smiling.

"No," he assured her with a hung head.

"Well, you shouldn't be. They said you were terrific."

"Terrific? I lost!"

"You never lost anything in your life, John Prichard."

"Oh, sure!" he added meekly.

"You haven't!" she stated.

"But you look tried to me," she continued, taking his arm. "Your trouble is you need someone looking out for you. Someone to take care of you."

"I do?"

"Yes, you do," she replied confidently. "And I'm going to do it. I'm going to fix you everything." By now they were walking home.

"Everything?" John asked.

"Yes, everything! Things pretty, things sweet, things new, things

old, things flat, round, square, just everything. Okra, cheese—"
"Okra!" John interrupted.
"Yes, okra and everything," she responded with glee. "You just wait and see."

Scripta humanistica

Directed by
BRUNO M. DAMIANI
The Catholic University of America
COMPREHENSIVE LIST OF PUBLICATIONS*

15. Bernardo Antonio González, *Parábolas de identidad: Realidad interior y estrategia narrativa en tres novelistas de postguerra.* $28.00
16. Carmelo Gariano, *La Edad Media (Aproximación Alfonsina).* $30.00
17. Gabriella Ibieta, *Tradition and Renewal in «La gloria de don Ramiro».* $27.50
18. *Estudios literarios en honor de Gustavo Correa.* Eds. Charles Faulhaber, Richard Kinkade, T.A. Perry. Preface by Manuel Durán. $25.00
19. George Yost, *Pieracci and Shelly: An Italian Ur-Cenci.* $27.50
20. Zelda Irene Brooks, *The Poetry of Gabriel Celaya.* $26.00
21. *La relación o naufragios de Alvar Núñez Cabeza de Vaca,* eds. Martin A. Favata y José B. Fernández. $27.50
22. Pamela S. Brakhage, *The Theology of «La Lozana andaluza.»* $27.50
23. Jorge Checa, *Gracián y la imaginación arquitectónica.* $28.00
24. Gloria Gálvez Lira, *Maria Luisa Bombal: Realidad y Fantasía.* $28.50
25. Susana Hernández Araico, *Ironía y tragedia en Calderón.* $25.00
26. Philip J. Spartano, *Giacomo Zanella: Poet, Essayist, and Critic of the «Risorgimento.»* Preface by Roberto Severino. $24.00
27. E. Kate Stewart, *Arthur Sherburne Hardy: Man of American Letters.* Preface by Louis Budd. $28.50
28. Giovanni Boccaccio, *The Decameron.* English Adaptation by Carmelo Gariano. $30.00
29. Giacomo A. Striuli, *«Alienation in Giuseppe Berto».* $26.50
30. Barbara Mujica, *Iberian Pastoral Characters.* Preface by Frederick A. de Armas. $33.00
31. Susan Niehoff McCrary, *«'El último godo' and the Dynamics of the Urdrama.»* Preface by John E. Keller. $27.50
32. *En torno al hombre y a sus monstruos: Ensayos críticos sobre la novelística de Carlos Rojas,* editados por Cecilia Castro Lee y C. Christopher Soufas, Jr. $31.50
33. J. Thomas O'Connell, *Mount Zion Field.* $24.50
34. Francisco Delicado, *Portrait of Lozana: The Lusty Andalusian Woman.* Translation, introduction and notes by Bruno M. Damiani. $39.50
35. Elizabeth Sullam, *Out of Bounds.* Foreword by Michael Cooke. $23.50
36. Sergio Corsi, *Il «modus digressivus» nella «Divina Commedia»* $28.75
37. Juan Bautista Avalle-Arce, *Lecturas (Del temprano Renacimiento a Valle Inclán).* $28.50
38. Rosendo Díaz-Peterson, *Las novelas de Unamuno.* Prólogo de Antonio Carreño. $30.00
39. Jeanne Ambrose, *Syntaxe Comparative Francais-Anglais.* $29.50

Forthcoming

* Carlo Di Maio, *Antifeminism in Selected Works of Enrique Jardiel Poncela.* $20.50

* Juan de Mena, *Coplas de los siete pecados mortales: Second and Third Continuations.* Ed. Gladys Rivera. $25.50
* Salvatore Calomino, *From Verse to Prose: The Barlaam and Josaphat Legend in Fifteenth-Century Germany.* $28.00
* Darlene Lorenz-González, *A Phonemic Description of the Andalusian Dialect Spoken in Almogía, Málaga — Spain.* $25.00
* Maricel Presilla, *The Politics of Death in the «Cantigas de Santa María.»* Preface by John E. Keller. Introduction by Norman F. Cantor. $27.50
* *Studies in Honor of Elias Rivers,* eds. Bruno M. Damiani and Ruth El Saffar. $25.00
* Godwin Okebaram Uwah, *Pirandellism and Samuel Beckett's Plays.* $28.00

BOOK ORDERS

* Clothbound. *All book orders,* except library orders, must be prepaid and addressed to **Scripta Humanistica**, 1383 Kersey Lane, Potomac, Maryland 20854. *Manuscripts* to be considered for publication should be sent to the same address.